Measures of Effectiveness for the Information-Age Army

RICHARD DARILEK   WALTER PERRY   JEROME BRACKEN
JOHN GORDON   BRIAN NICHIPORUK

Prepared for the United States Army

RAND   Arroyo Center

The research described in this report was sponsored by the United States Army, Contract No. DASW01-96-C-0004.

Library of Congress Cataloging-in-Publication Data

Measures of effectiveness for the information-age Army/Richard Darilek ... [et al.].
    p. cm
    "MR-1155-A."
    Includes bibliographical references.
    ISBN 0-8330-2847-2
    1. United States. Army. 2. Combat—Evaluation. 3. Combat—Data processing. 4.
Information warfare—United States. I. Darilek, Richard E.

UA25 .M43 2000
355.3'43—dc21

00-036615

RAND is a nonprofit institution that helps improve policy and decisionmaking through research and analysis. RAND® is a registered trademark. RAND's publications do not necessarily reflect the opinions or policies of its research sponsors.

Cover design by Tanya Maiboroda

Cover illlustration courtesy of Raytheon Command, Control and Communication Systems

Published 2001 by RAND
1700 Main Street, P.O. Box 2138, Santa Monica, CA 90407-2138
1200 South Hayes Street, Arlington, VA 22202-5050
RAND URL: http://www.rand.org/
To order RAND documents or to obtain additional information, contact Distribution Services: Telephone: (310) 451-7002; Fax: (310) 451-6915; Internet: order@rand.org

This report presents the results of a project sponsored by the Director of Strategy, Plans, and Policy, Office of the Deputy Chief of Staff for Operations and Plans, Department of the Army Staff. It reports on project research aimed at developing measures of effectiveness (MOEs) for ground forces in the Information Age. The objective of the project was to help the U.S. Army, in both its strategic planning and its operational research communities, begin to identify new MOEs that can capture the improved effectiveness expected to accrue to ground forces as they exploit Information-Age technologies.* As originally conceived by the sponsor, the purpose of the project was not to produce a full list of MOEs appropriate to the Army in the Information Age—or even the last word on the few we present—but, rather, to provide a firm foundation for their further development, as well as some prototypes.

This research was carried out in the Strategy, Doctrine, and Resources Program of RAND Arroyo Center, a federally funded research and development center sponsored by the United States Army.

---

*An early effort to define MOEs for the U.S. Army can be found in *Force Developments: The Measurement of Effectiveness*, USACDC Pamphlet No. 71-1, January 1973.

For more information on the RAND Arroyo Center, contact the Director of Operations, (310) 393-0411, extension 6500, or visit the Arroyo Center's Web site at *http://www.rand.org/organization/ard/*,

CONTENTS

FIGURES

TABLES

BACKGROUND

The 1990s have witnessed the dawn of what future historians will doubtless call the Information Age. It is clear that the ability to acquire, retrieve, manipulate, and exchange information has had and will continue to have a profound effect on a host of human activities. Warfare is no exception.

Although it is clear that information will have a far-reaching effect, quantifying or measuring that effect—how to do so—is far from well understood. Such an understanding is important to the Army, particularly at a time when it is spending a considerable amount of its scarce investment capital on establishing Information-Age links across its forces (the so-called digitization of the Army). As it transforms itself, the Army needs Information-Age analytic tools to help it make the best choices possible.

Chief among the analytic tools required are good measures of effectiveness (MOEs) that can demonstrate the value of information in terms of military outcomes. The current set of measures, such as force-exchange and territorial gains or losses, will continue to be useful, but they do not give much visibility to the growing contribution of information. Moreover, they are often calculated with simplistic head-on-head attrition models that omit important processes in which information plays a big role.

PURPOSE

This report develops a limited set of Information-Age MOEs in an attempt to spark the development of many more such measures, which will be needed in the future to quantify the value of information in military operations, including combat. *Joint Vision 2010* posited a series of new concepts of operations for the battlefield of the future: dominant maneuver, precision engagement, full-dimensional protection, and focused logistics. Although these concepts also reflect current operations, *Joint Vision 2010* contended that in the Information Age they become much more powerful—so much so that they are transformed, in effect, into new concepts. We draw on these *Joint Vision 2010* concepts and their further development in *Joint Vision 2020* to frame our exploration of the value of information or, more specifically, of information superiority, which is what the U.S. Army says, in *Army Vision 2010,* it seeks to achieve. In this work, we characterize information as knowledge. Knowledge differs from information in that it takes into account two key attributes of information: quality and value. As defined here, therefore, knowledge consists of relevant and useful information.

APPROACH

We first construct a probability model of knowledge. With this model serving as the theoretical basis for much of what follows, we return to the familiar and more traditional analytic tools of game theory and Lanchester equations to gain insights into the real effects of information on combat outcomes. Then we use these insights, as well as the probability model of knowledge, to develop various analytic relationships that support particular concepts of operations and that incorporate information metrics. Specifically, we develop a new knowledge-based MOE, battlespace control, for the concept of dominant maneuver. We also explore the feasibility of developing new MOEs for stability operations.

GAME THEORY

We employ game theory and then Lanchester equations to assess the value of information superiority, including the possibility of information dominance—i.e., information superiority so complete that it even affects what an opponent knows. The results of our game theory analysis show, among other things, that information makes an overwhelming contribution to the military outcome when one side achieves information dominance over the other, which we define as follows: one side (and not the other) knows the values of the strategic choices available to both sides, and that side also knows which strategy the other side will choose.

LANCHESTER EQUATIONS

The Lanchester equations provide another insightful way of gauging the contribution of information. When a strong information component is added to either the Lanchester square or the Lanchester linear law, it results in what we term a Lanchester "mixed" law. Increasing or decreasing the increments of information available to one side or the other, we found, can powerfully affect the way outcomes of a military engagement are calculated in terms of Lanchester's historical equations. Our calculation of combat outcomes reveals the following: a positive effect for the side acquiring additional information; a negative one for the side lacking or losing information; and formulas for expressing force ratios that change, during the course of the same engagement, from either square or linear law formulations in the beginning to some form of Lanchester "mixed" law in the end.

Our Lanchester-law discussions are, of course, simplifications. More serious combat modeling must resort to simulation. However, analogous effects should be visible in combat simulations if they properly reflect information asymmetries. To put the matter otherwise, our work would suggest that simulations should be tested to assure that they have reflected information asymmetries well enough to bring out the kinds of effects we discuss in this report.

MEASURES OF EFFECTIVENESS FOR COMBAT OPERATIONS

Of the four new concepts advanced by *Joint Vision 2010,* we focus on two: dominant maneuver and full-dimensional protection. For each, we develop MOEs and associated metrics and portray the effects of information mathematically. For these two concepts, Table S.1 shows the following:

- The MOEs;
- The metrics used to calculate these MOEs traditionally, where such metrics already exist; and
- The new, Information-Age metrics we have derived, for the most part by developing a way to calculate the knowledge factor discussed above and including it in every case as part of the metric.

The mathematical calculations show that as the ratio of relative knowledge changes, i.e., what one force knows relative to what the other force knows, outcomes swing in favor of the side with greater relative knowledge. For example, if one side is deploying forces to engage an opponent and discovers that the opponent has blocked certain avenues of approach, those can be avoided, thus speeding the arrival of side one's forces and increasing the amount of operational reach available to them.

Table S.1

Measuring Dominant Maneuver and Full-Dimensional Protection

Concept	MOE	Traditional Metric	Information-Age Metric
Dominant maneuver	Deployment	Items moved per unit of time	Knowledge of enemy attempts to block routes
	Operational reach	Kilometers per unit of time	Knowledge of enemy resistance along routes of advance
	Battlespace control		Size of unit control radius and speed of unit, plus relative knowledge
	FLOT movement	Kilometers	Knowledge of combat capability
Full-dimensional protection	Protection from direct and indirect fires	Hardness, deception and mobility	Knowledge-enhanced hardness, deception, and mobility
	Casualties	Number of losses	Number of losses

BATTLESPACE CONTROL MOE

Battlespace control, which is listed in Table S.1 as an MOE for the concept of dominant maneuver, represents a nontraditional measure made possible, in part, by the knowledge component of its Information-Age metrics. As Figure S.1 shows, we calculate this battlespace-control MOE as the product of a variety of factors: not only a relative knowledge factor but also an agility factor (to take into account a unit's movement speed) and a geometry factor, which accounts for the unit's control radius (itself a product of the ranges of that unit's organic sensors and weapon systems).

MEASURES OF EFFECTIVENESS FOR STABILITY OPERATIONS

In examining stability operations, we sorted among the 16 types listed in current joint doctrine and chose humanitarian assistance as

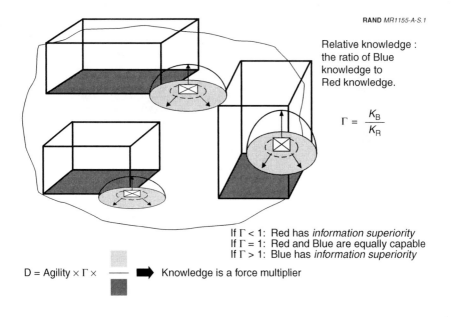

RAND *MR1155-A-S.1*

Relative knowledge : the ratio of Blue knowledge to Red knowledge.

$$\Gamma = \frac{K_B}{K_R}$$

If Γ < 1: Red has *information superiority*
If Γ = 1: Red and Blue are equally capable
If Γ > 1: Blue has *information superiority*

D = Agility × Γ × ⬛ ➡ Knowledge is a force multiplier

Figure S.1—The Effect of Knowledge

the exemplar for which to develop trial MOEs. We chose this example because the Army has a fair amount of recent experience in such operations, because they typically involve a mix of political and military means to achieve goals, and because they routinely cause the Army to work with many types of actors, e.g., international organizations (IOs) such as the United Nations High Commission for Refugees (UNHCR) and non-governmental organizations (NGOs) such as the American Red Cross.

As we did for the combat MOEs, we drew on the *Joint Vision 2010* concepts as a framework for developing MOEs for stability operations, settling on dominant maneuver as the concept of operations and understanding local environments as the measure. Developing metrics for this MOE (and others like it) is inherently difficult because we are attempting to apply quantitative metrics to qualitative measures. The process becomes even more difficult in addressing humanitarian assistance, because few of the traditional warfighting metrics apply. The metric we develop consists of the contribution of knowledge, as defined earlier, to the degree of understanding of the local environment.

Our approach is to break the "local environment" down into an number of constituent components (e.g., local government, history, terrain), ascertain where knowledge is deficient, and then identify how knowledge can contribute to stability. The theory is that the better the forces understand the local environment, the less likely they are to make errors that alienate the population and the more likely the mission is to succeed.

CONCLUDING OBSERVATIONS AND POTENTIAL IMPLICATIONS

This work on MOEs and associated metrics suggests strongly that information—in particular, information superiority—can have a powerful effect on the outcomes of military operations. The degree of information superiority that one side might be able to achieve over the other is what most needs to be measured in the Information Age. Thus, we have focused in this report on relative measures beginning with relative knowledge, for which we developed the knowledge metric. This metric expresses the relationship between ideal and actual knowledge, for both sides, in military operations. We have also focused here on the need for new MOEs to assess the new concepts of operation being embraced by the Army, as well as on the contribution that information can make to these and other concepts. This work, which is only the first step in a new direction along the road to the future, suggests that development of Information-Age, knowledge-based MOEs is feasible, not only for combat operations but for stability operations as well.

ACKNOWLEDGMENTS

The authors wish to acknowledge the invaluable contributions made to this report, in various stages of its preparation, by Paul Davis and Jerry Sollinger of RAND and by Dan Shedlowski and LTC Robert Steinrauf of the U.S. Army's Center for Army Analysis. Thanks are also due to Karen Echeverri for her extraordinary staff support in the preparation of this document for review and publication. The illustration used in the cover was provided by Raytheon Command, Control and Communication Systems, and we gratefully acknowledge their generous permission to reproduce it.

Chapter One

INTRODUCTION

The 1990s marked the dawn of the Information Age, a challenging successor to the Industrial Age that held sway throughout the 20th century. Improvements in technology are creating an ever-widening worldwide network of information sources, archives, consumers, and architectures. This worldwide network of information systems is increasingly interactive, producing an unprecedented level of communication, exchange, and interconnectivity that crosses organizational and national lines.

For this new age, the Army has to design and build a force capable of performing land-power missions. The Army is about to spend a substantial portion of its procurement budget on Information-Age linkages across its forces (e.g., the so-called digitization of Army XXI). Potential adversaries will probably make similar investments, while the U.S. Army will advance still farther into the Information Age (e.g., with the Army After Next). It needs new analytic methods to help accomplish this task: to evaluate future land-power concepts and to assess the tradeoffs between or among potentially competing concepts and their associated force structures.

In short, the Army needs analytic tools appropriate to the new challenges posed by the Information Age. Chief among these are new measures of effectiveness (MOEs) and their associated metrics that address unique features of this age. This project seeks to help spark the development of such new, increasingly relevant, ultimately necessary measures.

BACKGROUND

The basic force components—units and weaponry—currently used by both intelligence analysts and military modelers to measure force effectiveness will have to change as a result of the Information Age. Technological advances, such as new command, control, communications, computers, intelligence, and reconnaissance (C4ISR) systems and "internetting" across Army units, may produce major improvements in force effectiveness that will not even register in traditional Industrial-Age measures of combat outcomes.

New assessment yardsticks will be required to measure Information-Age improvements in our own forces, as well as the effectiveness of threat forces, given that our potential adversaries are also likely to invest in the new technologies. New MOEs and metrics should help guide the Army's search for the best technological applications, in addition to assessing applications already under development. Without MOEs that measure the presumed benefits of Information-Age technologies—*information superiority* and *dominant maneuver*, to name two—the Army's ability to guide and justify its own expenditures, or measure the real power of likely adversaries, will suffer.

Because traditional MOEs remain grounded in force-on-force models that calculate effectiveness on the basis of exchange ratios dominated by major weapon platforms, they measure only a portion of the capabilities a force is expected to bring to battle in the Information Age. Moreover, traditional MOEs already fall short when it comes to addressing stability and security operations, formerly known as military operations other than war (MOOTW), which could dominate military operations in the future.

Planning efforts both for the Army and for the Department of Defense as a whole have focused increasingly on information—its technologies and their organization—as key to the longer-term future. This focus is evident in such publications as the DoD's *Joint Vision 2010*, *Joint Vision 2020*, and the Army's TRADOC Pamphlet 525-5, *Force XXI Operations*,[1] and the 1997 and 1998 reports to the Chief of Staff of the Army on the Army After Next Project.[2] Army

---

[1] U.S. Department of the Army (1994). See also Perry and Millot (1988).

[2] U.S. Department of the Army (1997) and (1998).

warfighting experiments (AWEs) within the Force XXI process have also paid particular attention and devoted considerable resources to the potential benefits that increasing reliance on information promises to provide.

Twentieth-century "linear" MOEs, such as FLOT movement and force ratios, should remain relevant to Army XXI. That force, however, will also benefit from the incorporation of 21st-century technologies and subsystems, most of which relate to improvements in information. It stands to reason, therefore, that such developments may call forth additional measures—i.e., MOEs more directly attuned to Army XXI's particular Information-Age capabilities.

The development of MOEs for the Army After Next (AAN) is both more challenging and more tentative. Some of the measures that apply to current or Army XXI units will probably still be valid measures for AAN-era organizations. On the other hand, new equipment and organizations that break dramatically with the past could result in the need for new and different measures of effectiveness. New measures, in turn, could help guide the search for additional applications of information technologies, as well as the allocation of resources to that search.

Coming up with such new MOEs is a challenge to the entire analytic community.

APPROACH

Before addressing the development of new Information-Age MOEs, it is important to understand how we expect information to affect future military operations. This leads us inevitably to questions such as: What is information? How can it be measured? How do we assess its value?[3] These questions are not new, but they are becoming

---

[3]Alan Washburn of the Naval Postgraduate School at Monterey, California, makes two important points about the value of information: "Information has no value unless there is an uncertain decision maker," and "Information has no value unless the decision maker has the power to use it" (A. R. Washburn, *Bits, Bangs or Bucks? The Coming Information Crisis*, Naval Postgraduate School Paper at *http://web.nps.navy.mil/ ~orfacpag/resumePages/washburn/infoval.pdf.* Web page was accessed and available on October 19, 2000.)

increasingly important as we transition to a more information-dependent Army.[4]

The approach we have taken in this report is to present new Information-Age metrics based on our understanding of how information affects military operations. In doing this, we drew on backgrounds in military affairs and other domains such as physics, chemistry, and business. The "force ratio" concept is an example of a longstanding and well-understood metric that is used to measure combat outcome. In other domains we think, for example, of how powerful the related concepts of half-life and relaxation time have proved to be. They, like the force ratio, allow us to reflect simply on the bottom-line consequences of what may be extremely complex underlying phenomena (e.g., nonequilibrium chemistry, radioactive decay, turbulent flows settling into laminar flows and "learning curves" in industry). We thought also of "delay times," "confidence levels," and network-centric "leveraging."

We have searched for analogous analytical concepts that might prove useful in reflecting the implications of information in military operations. Our report is speculative, exploratory, and long on theory, but we hypothesize a number of analytical relationships that seem worthy of follow-on inquiry. By so doing, we hope to contribute to a continuing learning process that will help the Army discover how best to frame information issues in its analysis, doctrinal rules of thumb, and other domains.

OUTLINE

In Chapter Two we address the most important questions: What is information, and how do we measure it? We suggest that the important notion of information superiority, which the Army aspires to, can be expressed in terms of *knowledge*. We seek to ascertain, through further exploration of this broad concept, how much of it might be required by the Army in the future, as well as what the potential effects of such superiority might be. Following Chapter

---

[4]Early attempts to define a measure of information were made by communications theorists such as Nyquist (1924) and Hartley (1928) and by the statistician Fisher (1925). In 1948, Claude Shannon laid the broadest and most central foundation of information theory in his paper, "A Mathematical Theory of Communications."

Two, which establishes the theoretical basis for much of what is to come, the remainder of the report divides implicitly into two sections. The first, which comprises Chapters Three and Four, features exploratory research on the potential effects of knowledge as it ranges from superiority up to and including information dominance. The second section, which contains Chapters Five, Six, and Seven, addresses new MOEs based on the probability model of knowledge developed in Chapter Two. In Chapters Three and Four, we rely on the familiar and more traditional analytic tools of game theory[5] and Lanchester[6] equations to gain insights into the real effects of information on combat outcomes. In Chapters Five through Seven, we use these insights to develop various analytic relationships that incorporate information metrics and that support particular concepts of operations. Chapter Eight features concluding observations and potential implications of the report for the Army, which continues to search for new MOEs while coming to grips with an Information-Age future that has, in many respects, already begun.

---

[5]See Luce and Raiffa (1957).
[6]See Taylor (1983).

Chapter Two

A PROBABILITY MODEL OF KNOWLEDGE

The appropriate place to begin a discussion of Information-Age measures is with a discussion of information and how it affects military operations. Information has always been an integral part of military operations, from the earliest days of organized combat to today's modern armies. Commanders have always devoted considerable resources to improving intelligence reconnaissance and surveillance techniques while attempting to protect information about their own forces from the enemy through concealment and deception. The assumption is that the more a commander knows about the situation on the battlefield—especially what he knows about the enemy forces—the better he is able to employ his forces and therefore prevail.[1] Indeed, there are several historical examples that bear this out. In discussing cyberwar, for example, Arquilla and Ronfeldt describe how 12th-century Mongols used information to prevail against superior armies.

> Mongol doctrine relied for success almost entirely on learning exactly where their enemies were, while keeping their own whereabouts a secret until they attacked. This enabled them, despite chronic inferiority in numbers, to overthrow the finest, largest armies of Imperial China, Islam, and Christendom.[2]

---

[1]This generally implies that the commander is willing and able to act on the information made available to him, that is, it is possible for a commander to go down to defeat knowing a great deal about the enemy and friendly situation. In this work, we assume that information of value will be acted upon.

[2]Arquilla and Ronfeldt (1993).

Unfortunately, little has been done to establish a clear relationship between information and the outcome of military operations.[3] Part of the problem is that, unlike combat power, it is difficult to understand the many ways information affects military operations. For example, suppose the friendly ground commander knows the location of only 30 percent of the enemy forces. There are several situation-dependent actions he might take:

- If he has a large array of weapons with a commensurably large stockpile of ammunition, he might target the known 30 percent with precision weapons and attack other "hunch" locations with area weapons. In this case, the limited knowledge would result in 30 percent or more of the enemy's force destroyed—a "good" outcome.

- If he feels that his combat power is inferior to the enemy's, or that he has insufficient weapons to guarantee the destruction of the known 30 percent of the enemy force, he may choose to avoid combat until he can obtain more weapons and more information or until he achieves some other tactical advantage. This outcome is favorable to the enemy in that the enemy commander might take advantage of the delay to launch his own attack.

- If he has just enough combat power to destroy the entire enemy force, he may wish to delay until more information is available on the disposition of the other 70 percent of the enemy force in the hope that he can "make every shot count." As in the previous case, delay could favor the enemy.

If we add what the enemy commander knows, several other possibilities arise. The point is that there appears to be no tidy relationship between information available to the commander and the best way to proceed. Several other factors need to be assessed. However, this does not mean that we can do nothing. There are several "first principles" that can be extracted by examining some special cases.

---

[3]One attempt is reported in Perry and Moffat (1997). However, combat outcome is measured only in terms of enemy and friendly attrition. The use of information to avoid combat or to achieve other objectives was not explored.

KNOWLEDGE, IGNORANCE, AND VALUE

Information has two important attributes, *value* and *quality*. Information has value if it informs the commander and thereby adds to his knowledge of the combat situation. Consequently, when we refer to "knowledge" we really mean relevant and therefore "valuable" information. Information quality depends upon its accuracy, timeliness, and completeness. It is not always the case, therefore, that valuable information, or knowledge, is of high quality. Conversely, quality information may have little or no value, i.e., it may be extraneous information of scant utility and thus may even detract from knowledge.

In gathering information from sensors and sources, the commander seeks information that has value, usually expressed in terms of critical elements of information (CEI). The problem is that he is rarely able to accurately assess the quality of the information he receives. Consequently, he must generally assume that part of what he "knows" may be inaccurate. Continuing with the simple example above, the valuable information to the friendly commander is the location of the enemy forces. We asserted in the example that he "knows" the location of 30 percent of those forces. We said nothing about the quality of that information. Suppose now that the enemy was capable of using sophisticated deception techniques so that only half of the known forces are actually where the friendly commander thinks they are. This raises several issues with respect to the decisions the commander might make. If he suspects he is being deceived, he may choose to wait in all cases until more reliable (i.e., quality) information is available. If he does not suspect, then he may act as before, producing different, and perhaps less desirable, outcomes.

This suggests a useful information taxonomy. Suppose we let K be the measure of valuable information or knowledge available to the commander. In some cases, K may be a simple count, as in the preceding example. If the enemy force consists of N targetable entities (units, say), then $K = .3N$. That is, the commander knows the location of $.3N$ of the enemy units. For both sides, then, K has two components: knowledge that is of high quality and knowledge that is of little or no quality, and $K = K_c + K_i$. In the example, $K_c = K_i = .15N$. Typically, K is multidimensional, consisting of several information elements such as enemy posture, unit(s) identifications, etc. It is important to note with all of this that the commander most likely does not know he is being deceived and therefore this construct, although it may be useful for analysis, must be used cautiously.

A MEASURE OF KNOWLEDGE

In a combat area of operations (AO), gaining knowledge is as much a contest as is maneuver and the effective application of firepower. Once a unit arrives in the area of operations, we can expect it to be configured for offensive or defensive operations. The enemy is now a full player, actively attempting to achieve its objectives and, at the same time, prevent the friendly forces from achieving theirs. For this reason, we consider relative measures beginning with *relative knowledge*. We start with three definitions:

Definition 1: A unit *controls* an area when it is able to operate within the area at will. This does not imply that the enemy is excluded from the area, only that the friendly unit is able to exert its influence at will at all points in the area and at all times.

Definition 2: The *unit control radius* is the minimum of the following: the maximum effective range of the unit's organic and supporting indirect-fire weapon systems, w_i, the maximum effective range of its organic and supporting sensor systems, s_i, and the radius of its assigned area of operations, c_i.[4] Mathematically, the control radius for unit i, r_i is $r_i = \min \{w_i, s_i, c_i\}$.

Definition 3: *Knowledge* is the degree to which a unit commander has cognizance of enemy and friendly force dispositions within its control radius, i.e., has *situational awareness*. We denote unit knowledge for Blue unit i and Red unit j as $K_{B,i}$ and $K_{R,j}$, respectively.

Situational awareness in Definition 3 can be equated to knowledge about the CEI and would include such problematic elements as assessments of enemy posture and intent. The CEI or relevant information elements are the ingredients needed to formulate the

---

[4]The control radii for opposing sides are independent of each other.

common picture of the battlespace, and the degree to which this picture is clear to the unit commander constitutes his situational awareness, or knowledge.[5]

A Probability Model

Although knowledge is multidimensional, for purposes of this discussion we will continue to assume that a single element of information constitutes the CEI. Expanding the discussion to include the multidimensional case just complicates the mathematics while obscuring the message.[6] Continuing with the earlier example, we assume that the CEI consists only of the location of the enemy targets (or a critical subset of them, such as the location of all artillery batteries). Suppose, for example, the friendly commander has intelligence information indicating that there are n critical enemy targets. We let U represent the number of units located within the control radius $U \in \{0, 1, 2, \ldots, n\}$. U then is a random variable and $P(U = u)$ is the probability that u targets have been located within the control radius.

The initial distribution on U depends upon the information available to the commander from his sensors and sources. On initial deployment, the information available is generally provided by the initial preparation of the battlefield (IPB) process. In the worst case, no information on the location of enemy units is available and therefore $P(U = u) = 1/(n + 1)$, that is, it is equally likely that any number of enemy units, up to n, are located within his control radius. As additional sensor reports arrive, the probability distribution is refined. Ideally, the final distribution assigns probability 1 for $U = \mu$ and 0 for $U \neq \mu$. In reality, however, it may be the case that the location of several of the units (targets) will not be known with certainty in time for the commander to make a decision.

---

[5]We may learn of enemy intent directly from sources and sensors, or it may be inferred from the knowledge the commander has about enemy force dispositions.

[6]For example, location of a unit can be modeled as a bivariate normal distribution. Unit type can be estimated by comparing equipment counts against templates. The equipment counts are binomial, but because several pieces of equipment comprise a unit type, the resulting distribution is multinomial. These concepts will be more fully developed in forthcoming RAND research by W. Perry and T. Sullivan on "Modeling Information Processing with Implications for JWARS."

Before proceeding further, it is useful to examine some of the important factors that affect the probability distribution on **U**:

1. **The number of confirming reports.** Multiple confirming reports on the location of enemy targets tend to concentrate all of the probability on some fixed number of units in the control radius, u_f, so that $P(U = u_f) \to 1$ and $P(U \neq u_f) \to 0$.

2. **The number of disconfirming reports.** Disconfirming reports increase uncertainty, especially if the reports are from equally reliable sources. The effect on $P(U = u)$ is that it tends to "flatten," the worst case being $P(U = u) = 1/(n + 1)$. Both this phenomenon and the first factor are included in the formulation of the knowledge metric below.

3. **The reliability of the sensors and sources.** In some cases, the assessment of reliability is subjective, especially with human intelligence sources (HUMINT). Sensor platforms generally have an engineered reliability that varies with environmental conditions. Unreliable reports tend to be discounted and even ignored. The effect on $P(U = u)$ is then the same as in the second factor.

4. **Terrain occlusions.** Sensors and sources requiring clear fields of "vision" are severely degraded by terrain occlusions. The effect is to reduce the number of reports, therefore slowing the convergence of $P(U = \mu)$.[7]

5. **Multiple phenomenology.** Confirming reports on units from different sensor types increases the reliability of the reported locations and therefore speeds convergence of $P(U = \mu)$.

6. **The age of the information received.** The lack of recent reports reverses the convergence effects of any previous reports on the location of the enemy targets—especially if we assume that we are confronting a maneuvering enemy.

---

[7]The term "convergence" is used to mean that the probability distribution $P(U = u)$ changes only slightly from one sensor report to another.

Evaluating Sensor Reports

This suggests that we must next examine how the sensor reports refine the probability distribution on U. We begin by letting $V = \{0, 1, 2, \ldots, n\}$ represent the number of enemy units in the friendly commander's control radius whose location has been reported by the sensor suite. V is also taken to be a random variable, and $P(V = v)$ is the probability that the number of units within the control radius located by the sensor suite is v. However, this number is conditioned on the (unknown) number of enemy units in the control radius, μ. Consequently, we focus on $P(V = v \mid U = \mu)$ for $\mu \leq n$.[8] If we assume that the sensor reporting is capable of locating each single enemy target with probability q, then the conditional probability is binomial with distribution[9]

$$P(V = v \mid U = \mu) \equiv b(v;\mu,q) = \binom{\mu}{v} q^v (1-q)^{\mu-v} \text{ for } v = 0, 1, \ldots, \mu.$$

We next assume that the commander must make a decision within some period of time, thus limiting the number of sensor reports that can be used to refine the initial probability distribution. If we further assume that sensor reports are processed as they arrive, then $P_i(U = \mu \mid V = v)$ for all $\mu = 0, 1, \ldots, n$ at the ith sensor report is given by Bayes' formula:

$$P_i(U = \mu \mid V = v) = \frac{P_{i-1}(U = \mu)b(v;\mu,q)}{\sum_{u=0}^{n} P_{i-1}(U = u)b(v;u,q)},$$

---

[8]It is possible, of course, to have $\mu > n$ provided that we allow for false reports. The Poisson distribution would be appropriate in this case. For simplicity, we omit this complication here. See Perry and Moffat (1997) for a complete treatment of false targets in the same context.

[9]This construct can easily be adapted to accommodate varying levels of resolution. At the lowest level, q is a composite probability representing the combined probability that all sensors and sources can detect a target. At a higher level, we let q_i be the probability that sensor i detects a single target. Both levels are amenable to the updating and knowledge calculations that follow.

where the prior probability for the ith sensor report is $P_{i-1}(U = \mu) = P_{i-1}(U = \mu | V = v)$. In this formulation, a sensor report consists of an estimate on the location of v targets within the control radius.

Information Entropy Model

As each sensor report is processed, the commander's knowledge changes as reflected in the changing probability distribution, $P_i(U | V = v)$. A useful way to measure the current amount of knowledge is through the use of information entropy or "Shannon information."[10] Information entropy is a measure of the average amount of information in a probability distribution and is defined as

$$H[P_i(U|V = v)] = H_i(U|V = v) = \sum_{u=0}^{n} P_i(U = u|V = v) \ln[P_i(U = u|V = v)].$$

The entropy function is maximized when the information in the probability distribution is at its lowest (greatest level of uncertainty). Operationally, this occurs when the friendly commander has no sensor assets to deploy and no prior knowledge of the location of any of the n enemy targets. In this case, we have $P_0(U = u) = 1/(n + 1)$. It is easy to verify that the entropy in this distribution is $H_0(U) = \ln(n + 1)$. Conversely, if the ith sensor report confirms, with certainty, the location of μ units within the control radius, then $P_i(U = \mu | V = v) = 1$ and $P_i(U \neq \mu | V = v) = 0$. It is also easy to verify that the entropy in this distribution is 0. At any sensor report, the degree of certainty in the updated probability distribution is $\ln(n + 1) - H_i(U | V = v)$. Knowledge can then be measured using the normalized form of certainty, or[11]

$$K_i(U|V = v) = \frac{\ln(n+1) - H_i(U|V = v)}{\ln(n+1)}.$$

---

[10]For a discussion of information entropy, see Blahut (1988).

[11]The author has referred to this formulation for knowledge as "residual knowledge," reflecting the fact that it is based on the converse of the remaining uncertainty in the probability distribution. See Perry and Moffat (1997). In subsequent discussions, we drop the argument on K.

More important than knowing the location of the n targets within the control radius is knowing the number of enemy targets in the jth target area of interest (TAI). Figure 2.1 depicts a control area with three TAIs. If, in ground truth, the number of enemy targets in each is μ_j, then we have that $\sum_j \mu_j \leq n$. For simplicity, we assume that the TAIs do not overlap so that knowledge is the sum of the knowledge the friendly unit commander has about the location of the enemy targets within the TAIs. In this case, $K = \sum_{j=1}^{3} \omega_j K_j$, where K_j is the knowledge gained on the location of targets in TAI$_j$, and ω_j is the relative importance placed on TAI$_j$ by the friendly commander $\left(\sum_{j=1}^{3} \omega_j = 1\right)$. A nonweighted average is also possible so that $K = \frac{1}{3} \sum_{j=1}^{3} K_j$. The knowledge metric in this case is a weighted average over the TAIs and represents the commander's level of situational awareness.

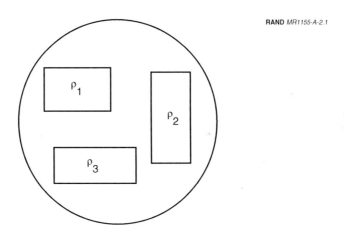

RAND *MR1155-A-2.1*

Figure 2.1—Control Radius TAIs

Relative Knowledge

Returning now to our original definitions, we have that the "side" knowledge is the average of the side's unit knowledge, or

$K_B = \frac{1}{m}\sum_{i=1}^{m} K_{Bi}$ and $K_R = \frac{1}{s}\sum_{i=1}^{s} K_{Ri}$. Relative knowledge or relative situational awareness is then defined to be the ratio of the two, or

$$\Gamma = \frac{K_B}{K_R}, K_R \neq 0.$$

Note that the ratio, Γ, is unbounded from above and bounded by 0 from below.

INFORMATION SUPERIORITY

There is an expectation (fairly widespread) that the Information-Age Army of the future will enjoy *information superiority*—and the more specific question is how much information superiority the Army might need to enjoy in order to be effective in that future. A "vision" of information superiority pervades *AV 2010*, in which such superiority is defined as the "capability to collect, process, and disseminate an uninterrupted flow of information while exploiting or denying an adversary's ability to do the same."[12]

By defining relative knowledge, Γ, as above, we have a way to assess relative information superiority between Red and Blue. Table 2.1 summarizes the possible relationships. The question of "how much information superiority is enough" is addressed next.

Table 2.1

Relative Knowledge

If ...	then ...	and ...
$K_B > K_R$	$\Gamma > 1$	Blue has information superiority.
$K_B < K_R$	$\Gamma < 1$	Red has information superiority.
$K_B = K_R$	$\Gamma = 1$	There is no information advantage.

[12]For a discussion of "information superiority" and "information dominance," see *Army Vision 2010*, p. 17, and *Concept for Future Joint Operations: Expanding Joint Vision 2010*, May 1997, Chapter 5.

INFORMATION DOMINANCE

Unlike information superiority, the meaning of *information dominance* is less clear. Other than to state that information operations (IO) are conducted to gain information dominance, *AV 2010* is vague about just what it means, except to state that

> [IO] consists of both offensive and defensive efforts to create a disparity *between what we know about our battlespace and operations within it and what the enemy knows about his battlespace.* (Emphasis added.)

It would appear that information dominance is achieved when the "disparity" between Blue and Red knowledge is sufficiently large. An information-gap definition of dominance implies that for Blue to enjoy information dominance, the difference between Blue and Red knowledge exceeds some threshold value. The relative-knowledge metric can also be used to define information dominance by defining values for Γ that correspond to the requisite difference between the two side's knowledge metrics. Suppose we let $0 < \beta < 1$ be the requisite gap to ensure information dominance. For Blue to enjoy information dominance, then, we must first have that $K_B > K_R$ (information superiority is a prerequisite for information dominance)[13] and that $1 \geq K_B - K_R \geq \beta$. Dividing both sides by K_R gives us the inequality

$$\frac{1}{K_R} \mp 1 \geq \frac{\beta}{K_R}.$$

---

[13]The requirement that a side, to enjoy information dominance, must first achieve information superiority is not true in all cases. It is possible that a side's information needs are very low and that it may, with very little information, achieve information dominance without information superiority. Examples are Vietnam and Somalia. In Vietnam, for example, the Viet Cong required very little information compared to the United States and its allies and yet were able to dominate—at least locally. See Gritton et al. (1999). The authors define information dominance as "the concept that we have a decided advantage in situation awareness—not just that we obtain good information. We need to deny the enemy the ability to collect information and—if he does gather it—stop him from capitalizing on it." Note that there is no explicit discussion of information superiority. A side may enjoy an advantage in situation awareness with inferior knowledge.

This generates the following bounds on Γ:

$$1+\frac{\beta}{K_R} \lessgtr 1+\frac{1}{K_R}.$$

A similar calculation can be made to assess the bounds on Γ for Red information dominance. Therefore, given a requisite knowledge gap for information dominance, we can specify conditions on relative knowledge that must be met to ensure that dominance is maintained. Thus we infer a relationship between information superiority and information dominance.

It seems logical to discuss information dominance occurring at some point where one or both sides have knowledge that exceeds some threshold. That is, there is a qualitative difference between relative knowledge of $\Gamma = 2$ when $K_B = .01$ and $K_R = .005$ and when $K_B = .8$ and $K_R = .4$. Furthermore, we cannot assume that this threshold is the same for both Red and Blue. It may be that the two sides have different information requirements. If we set the threshold levels to be $0 < \delta_R, \delta_B < 1$ for Red and Blue respectively, then information dominance depends upon the relationship between K_B and K_R and between δ_B and δ_R. Figure 2.2 summarizes the various information dominance possibilities.

Note that in the "neither dominates" case, it is still possible for one or the other side to have information superiority when neither has information dominance. In the other two regions, either Blue or Red enjoys information superiority as well as information dominance.

The diagram helps to understand the relationship between information superiority and information dominance. If, as stated in *AV 2010*, information operations are used to gain information dominance by increasing the gap between Blue and Red knowledge, then we can see that Blue would use offensive operations to destroy, disrupt, and deceive Red C4ISR to move to the upper left of the diagram. Similarly, Red would do the same to move to the lower right. It is not clear just how useful this construct is in analysis. Assigning meaning to the fractional threshold values may be problematic. However, it is useful to illustrate the effects of information dominance in situations where one side or the other enjoys information superiority.

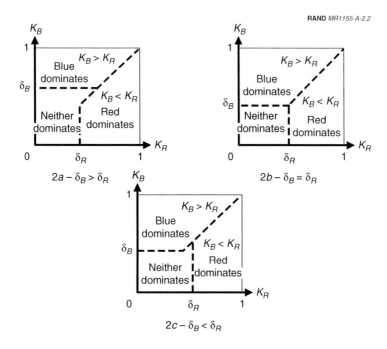

Figure 2.2—Information Dominance

In subsequent calculations, we use knowledge and relative knowledge to assess the effect of information superiority and dominance (or the lack of them) on an Information-Age measure of combat effectiveness.

Chapter Three

GAMING INFORMATION

Game theory has been widely used to analyze the effects of selecting alternative strategies to achieve a military objective.[1] In two-person zero-sum games, i.e., a payoff to player 1 is a loss to player 2, both players have several alternative strategies they may pursue and, although each is aware of the strategies available to his opponent, neither is aware of the strategy his opponent will select. Therefore each player may select a strategy that will maximize his minimum payoff. Such a player will hedge against the likelihood that his opponent will select the strategy that results in the worst payoff.[2] The effects of knowing about an opponent's strategy makes game theory an excellent place to start a discussion of the effects of information on combat outcomes (payoffs). We do this by allowing each of the players (actually, "sides" in a battle) to possess varying amounts of relevant information about the strategy his opponent will select, and then we measure the effect this has on the outcome of the game. In essence, we are postulating varying levels of K_B and K_R.

---

[1]For a discussion of game theory applied to the World War II Battle of the Bismark Sea, see Luce and Raiffa (1957), p. 64.

[2]There are other playing strategies, of course. A player may "go for the gold" by selecting the strategy that maximizes the *probability* of his maximum payoff. Although risky, it is nevertheless an option that has been used in past military campaigns with good success. Although this may increase the likelihood of a bad outcome, some historical generals have chosen to worry less about so-called expected outcomes than about doing everything they could to win. In part, probably, this has been due to their believing that one can make one's own luck. But there is also an important psychological component at work.

We have designed four games in which the amount of information possessed by each side (K_B and K_R) is allowed to vary. Side 1's information might be thought of, by analogy, as comparable to that available to the U.S. Army in

- The current force, the Army of Excellence (AOE) (Game 1);

- Army XXI (Game 2); and

- Army After Next[3] (AAN) (Games 3 and 4).

In addition to four different assumptions about the information available to both sides, we considered three cases of dimensionality with respect to the number of strategies or choices available to both sides. We allow each side three, five, or ten choices. (This feature of the game has some intuitive relationship with warfare, where the value of intelligence relates to the degrees of freedom available to opposing sides, which are usually rather limited.)

THE GAME

All the games have the structure depicted in Figure 3.1. Sides 1 and 2 have choices $i = 1, 2, \ldots, m$ and $j = 1, 2, \ldots, n$, respectively. For each pair of choices there is a payoff $a_{i,j}$. Side 1 receives $a_{i,j}$ and Side 2

RAND *MR1155-A-3.1*

Side 2 strategies (j)

$$
\begin{array}{c}
 & \begin{array}{cccc} 1 & 2 & \cdots & n \end{array} \\
\text{Side 1 strategies } (i) \begin{array}{c} 1 \\ 2 \\ \vdots \\ m \end{array} & \left[\begin{array}{cccc} a_{1,1} & a_{1,2} & \cdots & a_{1,n} \\ a_{2,1} & a_{2,2} & \cdots & a_{2,n} \\ \vdots & \vdots & \vdots & \vdots \\ a_{m,1} & a_{m,2} & \cdots & a_{m,n} \end{array} \right]
\end{array}
$$

Figure 3.1—Game Matrix

---

[3]See Perry and Millot (1998); also Perry, Pirnie, and Gordon (1999a, 1999b).

loses $a_{i,j}$. Side 1 therefore wishes to maximize the payoff and Side 2 wishes to minimize the payoff. This leads Side 1 to pursue what is referred to as a "maximin" strategy and Side 2 to pursue a "minimax" strategy.

Selecting the Optimal Strategy

Side 1's optimal strategy, i^*, is found by first computing, for each of his possible choices i, the worst outcome (the outcome that would come about if Side 2 made the best choice consistent with Side 1's having chosen i). We call that worst outcome $a_{i,\,min}$, which is given by

$$a_{i,\,min} = \min_{j}\,(a_{i,j}).$$

Side 1's most conservative choice, i^*, is the one that maximizes $a_{i,\,min}$. That is, he chooses the row for which $a_{i,\,min}$ is largest:

$$a_{max,\,min} = \max_{i}\,(a_{i,\,min}).$$

His payoff will then be at least as good as $a_{max,\,min}$.

For Side 2, we reverse the process. Side 2's optimal strategy, j^*, is found by first computing, for each of his possible choices j, the best outcome (the outcome that would come about if Side 1 made the best choice consistent with Side 2's having chosen j). We call that the worst outcome, $a_{max,\,j}$. It is given by

$$a_{max,\,j} = \max_{i}\,(a_{i,j}).$$

Now Side 2's most conservative choice, j^*, is the one that minimizes $a_{max,j}$. That is, he chooses the column for which $a_{max,\,j}$ is smallest:

$$a_{min,\,max} = \min_{j}(a_{max,\,j}).$$

His payoff will then be at least as good as $a_{min,\,max}$.

The Variable Knowledge Cases

We might think about war abstractly as follows. In any given battle, Side 1's choice of strategies will have some effect on the outcome, as will Side 2's. Depending on the circumstances of battle (force ratios, terrain, etc.), the strategies may make more or less difference. How, then, do we think about the value of information? As an abstraction, we can consider a vast array of battles in which strategies have very different consequences for the outcomes. We can then ask how much value information would have, on average, over that vast array of battles. This is indeed what we have calculated. For each of 1,000 different battles we generated a payoff matrix as in Figure 3.1, using random numbers between 0 and 100. We then made various assumptions about how much knowledge each side had about the payoff matrix. Each side then selected strategies based on that knowledge. We did this first assuming that the sides had three strategies each; we repeated the work with five and ten strategies. In the discussions below, we refer to the payoff matrix depicted in Figure 3.1 as **A**.

- **Game 1: current force (AOE) (both sides have correct information).** Side 1 and Side 2 have common and correct knowledge of all the values of the payoff matrix **A**. Both sides have the same information about payoffs but are ignorant about each other's choices. Neither has superior knowledge. This can be thought of as the case in which $K_B = K_R$ and $\Gamma = 1$.

- **Game 2: Army XXI (Side 1 has correct information and Side 2 has incorrect information).** Side 1 has correct knowledge of all the values of $\mathbf{A} = \mathbf{A}_1$, and Side 2 has a completely *incorrect* understanding of the payoff matrix. We simulate this by providing Side 2 with a payoff matrix, $\mathbf{A} = \mathbf{A}_2$, composed of a second set of random numbers between 0 and 100. Therefore Side 2 will make decisions based on erroneous information. Although purely an abstraction, this could describe a situation in which Army XXI with superb information fights an enemy who not only lacks valid information but is thoroughly confused. This can be thought of as the case in which Blue (Side 1) has information superiority, i.e., $K_B > K_R$ and $\Gamma > 1$.

- **Game 3: AAN (Side 1 has correct information, Side 2 has correct information, and Side 1 knows Side 2's choice).** Side 1 and Side

2 have correct knowledge of the values of **A**, as in Game 1. Side 2 chooses his minimax strategy j^* from the correct matrix **A**. Side 1, however, knows the choice Side 2 makes, and rather than choose his maximin strategy (i^*), he focuses only on the payoffs corresponding to the minimax choice of Side 2 and maximizes his payoff. This simulates the case in which Side 1 has perfect intelligence and, as a result, another kind or higher level of information superiority. Although Side 2's basic information in this case (as opposed to Game 2) is not bad, it is clearly inferior to Side 1's. In this case, we have again that $K_B > K_R$ and $\Gamma > 1$, but now Γ is significantly greater than 1.

- **Game 4: AAN (Side 1 has correct information, Side 2 has incorrect information, and Side 1 knows Side 2's choice).** In the fourth game Side 1 has correct knowledge of all the values of $\mathbf{A} = \mathbf{A}_1$ and Side 2 has a completely incorrect payoff matrix $\mathbf{A} = \mathbf{A}_2$ composed of a second set of random numbers between 0 and 100, as in Game 2. Side 2 chooses his minimax strategy, j^*, from the incorrect information in $\mathbf{A}_2$. Side 1 knows the choice of Side 2. Rather than using his maximin strategy, he focuses only on the payoffs corresponding to the minimax choice of Side 2 from the incorrect information and makes his choice from the correct matrix, $\mathbf{A}_1$. Side 1 has perfect information (maximum knowledge). He may even have established this position by actively ensuring (through offensive information operations) that Side 2 has bad information. Thus, Side 1 enjoys not only information superiority but also information dominance, i.e., $K_B > \delta_B$ and $K_B > K_R$.

RESULTS

Table 3.1 summarizes the results of the four games. In each case, three different sets of strategies, or game sizes, were involved. The entries in the table can be thought of as percentages reflecting the likelihood that Side 1 will be successful given the relative knowledge between the two sides. It is important to note that the table entries do not reflect the likelihood that Side 1 will experience a successful combat outcome, but rather the degree to which relative knowledge contributes to Side 1's successful outcome: relative force ratios, weapon system effectiveness, and other measures discussed later

Table 3.1

The Effect of Knowledge on Game Outcomes

Game Size	Game 1	Game 2	Game 3	Game 4
3×3	50	63	58	75
5×5	50	61	65	83
10×10	49	59	75	91

contribute as well. A score of 90, for example, means that relative knowledge contributed 90 percent to Side 1's successful outcome, whereas it contributed only 10 percent to Side 2's successful outcome. The actual outcome is not of interest here, just the contribution of knowledge.

The games reflect the effect of knowledge on the likelihood of a successful outcome. Beginning with Game 1, we see that, as predicted, when neither side enjoys information superiority, the likelihood of winning is even—that is, the contribution of knowledge to winning is even. This seems to hold regardless of the number of strategies available to each side. This also applies to Game 2, with Side 2 possessing erroneous information about the outcomes.

The pattern appears to change, however, for Games 3 and 4. There appears to be a greater advantage to Side 1 when the number of strategies increases. This phenomenon is easy to explain based on the structure of the game. Side 2's selections in both games approach random choices, where the probability of selecting any of the s strategies is $1/s$. Therefore, the likelihood of succeeding is greater for smaller strategy sets. What is not clear from all this is whether the seeming advantages associated with information superiority and large strategy sets is applicable to real-world engagements. What is missing is some understanding of the relative importance of the choices being made. We touch on this issue with the Gulf War example below.

What can be said is that these results suggest that control of information is a fairly decisive key to victory for the Army of the future. Correspondingly, lack of information superiority in the future could prove to be devastating to the side that finds itself in the inferior position.

Also implicit in these games is the notion that information superiority and dominance result from dynamic interactions between the two sides. These can change over time—e.g., during the course of a conflict. Hence, we should guard against thinking of information superiority or dominance as static conditions that, once obtained, endure indefinitely for one side or the other. Prudence suggests viewing them also as objectives to be achieved or restored temporarily.

INFORMATION IN THE GULF WAR

These games, of course, represent relatively simple, abstract calculations designed to stimulate qualitative insights. In lieu of harder, not-yet-available data on 21st-century Army choices, such games help demonstrate the potential contribution of information superiority and information dominance to victory, and they are consistent with the concept of relative knowledge developed in the previous chapter. Although they are instructive, the true test of the game-theory models is whether they offer us more insight than qualitative assessments about the value of information. For example, common sense might lead us to hypothesize that the value of information depends on the extent to which the outcome of battle depends on the choices of the combatants. If there is a huge disparity of forces, open terrain, and no opportunities for surprise or deception, perhaps the only choices available are relatively inconsequential. In contrast, if important choices are available to the antagonists, such as trades between surprising the opponent versus having more time to prepare (as in the example described in the previous chapter), or between concentrating in one sector rather than spreading forces uniformly, then information can be crucial.

The Gulf War provides an excellent forum to examine these issues.[4] Both General Schwarzkopf and Saddam Hussein had an array of choices available to achieve their objectives. The U.S.-led coalition (Side 1) set as its objective the extraction of Iraqi forces from Kuwait.

---

[4]U.S. Department of Defense (1992).

The Iraqis (Side 2), for their part, were determined to stay. The outcome of the conflict, therefore, is binary: the Iraqi forces leave Kuwait (desirable to Side 1 and undesirable to Side 2) or the Iraqi forces remain (desirable to Side 2 and undesirable to Side 1). We might easily populate the game matrix depicted in Figure 3.1 with each outcome based on the strategies selected by the antagonists. However, the U.S.-led coalition may also be interested in how long it takes to eject the Iraqis from Kuwait, and how completely it is able to do so. If we define as an outcome *the number of days required to completely eject the Iraqi forces from Kuwait*, the competing interests are clear. The Iraqis and the coalition understand that a prolonged conflict will weaken U.S. support for the operation. Therefore, it is in the interest of Baghdad to lengthen the conflict and it is in the interest of the coalition to shorten it. We can also accommodate failure to eject by assigning a prohibitively long time to a pair of choices.

The choices available to each side are described below. Although each choice was available to each side, it is not clear that either explicitly discussed them.

Coalition Choices

The following is a list of the coalition options in the Gulf War aimed at ejecting Iraqi forces from Kuwait. Figure 3.2 illustrates each.

1. **Flanking attack.** This is the option actually selected by the coalition. The main coalition ground offensive would be a huge flank attack intended to sweep west of Kuwait in the direction of the key Iraqi Republican Guard units that were positioned in northern Kuwait–southeast Iraq. Once the Republican Guard was defeated, the main Iraqi force in Kuwait would be encircled. Superior coalition situational awareness, coupled with the ability to navigate in the open desert west of Kuwait (due to GPS), facilitated the rapid coalition ground advance in the historical operation.

2. **Frontal attack.** This represents the option in which the coalition attacks directly into the Iraqi forces holding Kuwait, relying on superior training and firepower, as opposed to maneuver, to prevail. Although this option was not executed, much of the Coali-

tion deception effort sought to convince the Iraqis that this was the actual allied plan of attack.

3. **Flanking attack with supporting amphibious attack.** This assumes that in addition to the large VII Corps flanking maneuver west of Kuwait, Marine forces conduct an amphibious assault near the head of the Gulf. This operation was actually planned, but not carried out. The advantage of such a maneuver was that it could have presented Iraqi commanders with an additional threat in the northeast of the Kuwaiti theater of operations.

4. **Frontal attack with supporting amphibious attack.** This assumes that in addition to a large attack directly from Saudi Arabia into Kuwait, a Marine amphibious assault would have taken place. Such an assault would have created pressure on the northeast portion of the Iraqi force in Kuwait simultaneous with a major attack coming from the south.

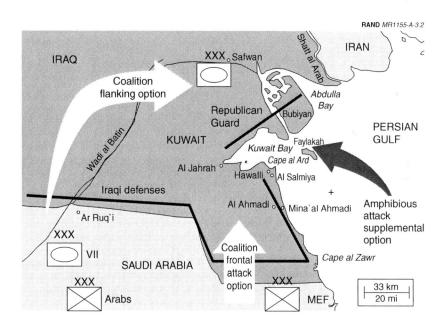

RAND *MR1155-A-3.2*

Figure 3.2—Coalition Offensive Options

Iraqi Choices

The following is a list of Iraqi options aimed at defending their occupation and control of Kuwait. Figure 3.3 illustrates each.

1. **Withdraw.** This option assumes that the Iraqis positioned themselves inside Kuwait specifically to conduct a fighting withdrawal in the event of a coalition ground attack to liberate the country. Iraqi forces would have been deeply arrayed throughout Kuwait in order to inflict casualties on the advancing coalition forces, particularly if the latter advanced directly from the south as in the coalition "frontal attack" option.

2. **Hold.** This option represents the plan that the Iraqis actually tried to implement. A large number of Iraqi infantry divisions were moved into southern Iraq and Kuwait and dug into the so-called Saddam Line. The Iraqi intent was to inflict maximum casualties on advancing coalition forces by having their troops fight from fortified positions. From the Iraqi perspective, this strategy was best suited to a coalition frontal attack from the south. Additionally, this option was intended to try to maintain Iraqi control of Kuwait.

3. **Maneuver to counterattack.** This option assumes that the Iraqis could have maintained sufficiently strong air defenses allowing their Republican Guard and other regular army armored forces to maneuver freely around the Kuwaiti theater of operations. Depending on whether the coalition elected to attempt a flank or frontal attack, with or without an associated amphibious assault, the Iraqis would use their large armored formations to aggressively maneuver and counterattack.

The Game Matrix

Arraying the coalition choices vertically and the Iraqi choices horizontally, we get the Side 1–Side 2 matrix depicted in Figure 3.4. The entries in the matrix are payoffs expressed in terms of the number of days required to eject the Iraqis from Kuwait. In this case, a lower number favors the coalition. A higher number favors the Iraqis; they reasoned that the longer the coalition fought, the greater its casualties, contributing to the erosion of support for the operation and

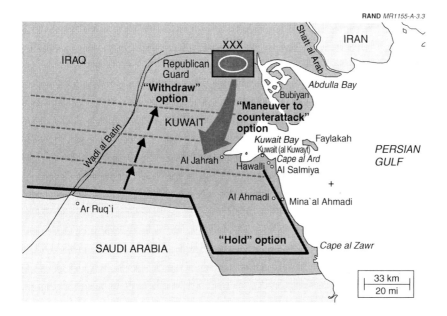

Figure 3.3—Iraqi Defensive Options

hopefully its termination. For the purposes of this example we assume that these numbers are fixed, so analysis consists of simply solving the single game.[5] An alternative would be to assume that these numbers are estimates of the average number of days required to eject Iraqi forces. We might further stipulate a probability distribution that reflects the uncertainty associated with the estimates. Analysis would then consist of solving several random games, as was done in the previous examples.

The actual outcome is seen at the intersection of a coalition flank attack and an Iraqi hold strategy. The result was the "100-hour" (i.e., four-day) ground offensive that resulted in the liberation of Kuwait. Note, however, that this matrix postulates that a coalition frontal attack opposed by an Iraqi hold strategy would have resulted in a

---

[5]We should also note that these numbers are approximations based on documentary evidence and conversations with colleagues familiar with the military art.

RAND *MR1155-A-3.4*

Iraqi defensive options

	1. Withdraw	2. Hold	3. Maneuver
1. Flank attack	7	4	7
2. Frontal attack	8	12	16
3. Flank attack w/amphib	6	3	8
4. Frontal attack w/amphib	7	8	10

Coalition offensive options

Figure 3.4—Game Matrix as Viewed by the Coalition

considerably longer amount of time to retake Kuwait. Additionally, it can be seen that a coalition amphibious assault would improve the coalition timeline, but not by a consistent amount. Finally, it is assumed that if the Iraqis could have maintained a sufficiently strong air defense network over Kuwait to permit a counterattack strategy against a coalition frontal attack, such a course of action would have resulted in the longest amount of coalition delay in retaking Kuwait.

In the first game, we assume that both sides know the payoffs. That is, both the coalition and the Iraqis have equivalent knowledge of the consequences of their strategic options in terms of days to eject, when countered by the opposing side's strategy choices. Note that the strategy that minimizes the coalition's losses is the flanking attack. This strategy requires, at worst, seven days to eject the Iraqi forces from Kuwait. For the Iraqis, however, the strategy that gains them the most time regardless of the coalition's strategy is to maneuver. At worst, this gives them seven days as well. Therefore, if both sides have knowledge of the game matrix, the outcome is seven days of combat to eject the Iraqis from Kuwait. In the Gulf War, Iraq chose to hold while the coalition chose to maneuver. The result was that the Iraqis were ejected in four days, as is depicted in the game matrix. Care must be taken not to read too much into this simple interpretation of the war. The reason the Iraqis chose to remain in place may have been for reasons other than knowledge about the number of days required to eject them from Kuwait.

Now let us assume that the coalition has successfully deceived the Iraqis so that their estimates of the number of days it will take to eject them from Kuwait are as depicted in Figure 3.5. The coalition sticks to the estimated ejection times depicted in Figure 3.4. The best strategy for the coalition is still a flank attack. However, based on their erroneous game matrix, the Iraqis opt to hold in place, reasoning that the worst they can do is delay ejection by 21 days and thus inflict unacceptable casualties on the coalition. In fact, by selecting this option, the actual number of days required was four. Therefore, the lack of information (if we believe that this misperception was what motivated the Iraqis to stay in their prepared positions) resulted in an unfavorable outcome for the Iraqis.

The matrix in Figure 3.5 reflects an incorrect Iraqi assessment of their options in relation to possible coalition strategies. For example, the Iraqis have concluded that they can easily cope with a coalition amphibious assault. The matrix reflects this, since it shows the (incorrect) Iraqi assessment that the addition of an amphibious assault does not improve the coalition's timeline to retake Kuwait. Additionally, the Iraqis have incorrectly concluded that a hold strategy on their part will result in longer delay for the coalition than a maneuver to counterattack course of action (the eventuality most feared by the coalition, based on its accurate assessment of possible courses of action). Essentially, the Iraqis have an overly optimistic view of their defensive capabilities in the hold option.

SOME IMPLICATIONS

From these simple game-theory experiments, we can begin to appreciate the effects of relative information superiority and dominance as reflected through knowledge in a tangible way. This suggests that we need to expend considerable effort on protecting our own C4ISR assets and capabilities and an equal amount on disrupt-

RAND *MR1155-A-3.5*

Iraqi defensive options

	1. Withdraw	2. Hold	3. Maneuver
1. Flank attack	5	21	14
2. Frontal attack	10	28	25
3. Flank attack w/amphib	5	21	14
4. Frontal attack w/amphib	10	28	25

Coalition offensive options

Figure 3.5—Game Matrix as Viewed by Iraq

ing the enemy's similar capabilities. Defensive and offensive C4ISR operations are generally referred to as information warfare (IW).[6] It is important, therefore, to measure how well we are able to perform these functions. This suggests two measures:

- **C4ISR protection** measures the degree to which the Army is able to conduct defensive operations that help it maintain or ensure information superiority. In the simple experiments described above, C4ISR protection clearly contributed to Side 1's ability, in every case, to know the values associated with its strategies.

- **C4ISR attack** measures the degree to which the Army is able to conduct offensive operations against an enemy's C4ISR assets and procedures. Offensive operations are aimed at degrading or penetrating an enemy's information capabilities. In Game 2 and Game 4, C4ISR attack might have been the means by which Side 2 lost its knowledge of the values associated with the strategies of

---

[6]The Army uses the broader term, information operations (IO), that encompasses routine operation of C4ISR systems as offensive and defensive actions. See Army Field Manual 100-6 and JCS Publication 3-13.

both sides. In Games 3 and 4, C4ISR attacks may have been the means by which Side 1 gained its knowledge of Side 2's choice of strategy.

In some ways, these two are the most important operations the Army can conduct in the Information Age. Being able to protect C4ISR systems against enemy attack is a *sine qua non* for obtaining the levels of information superiority needed to produce victorious results, such as those obtained in the games just presented. Successful attacks on enemy C4ISR—good offensive information operations— are also required to help translate such information superiority into information dominance.

Chapter Four

KNOWLEDGE-ENHANCED LANCHESTER

The Lanchester attrition processes are perhaps the best-known models of combat. They were developed by F. W. Lanchester just prior to U.S. involvement in World War I and were first published in his now famous book, *Aircraft in Warfare: The Dawn of the Fourth Arm*.[1] Lanchester distinguishes two forms of warfare: ancient and modern. The former is characterized by his linear law and the latter by his square law. In this chapter, we discuss both and present a third, information-enhanced variant which we refer to as the Lanchester *mixed law*. This third law is an attempt to assess the implications of information superiority for ground combat by referring to an established body of work other than game theory. Unit effectiveness, force survivability, and force size as well as force structure may change as a result of better information. The Lanchester laws provide a useful set of models to examine these changes.

Lanchester hypothesized basic "laws" that describe combat in "ancient times" and under "modern conditions." Taylor summarized Lanchester's laws as follows:

> In "ancient times," warfare was essentially a sequence of one-on-one duels so that the casualty-exchange ratio during any period of battle did not depend on the combatants' force levels. But under "modern conditions," however, the firepower of weapons widely separated in firing location can be concentrated on surviving targets so that each side's casualty rate is proportional to the number of

---

[1] Lanchester [1916] (1956).

enemy firers and the casualty-exchange ratio consequently depends inversely on the force ratio.[2]

The fundamental difference between ancient and modern warfare, then, is that in modern warfare there is a decided advantage to be gained from concentrating forces, whereas in ancient warfare there is no such advantage.[3] In ancient warfare, for example, if 1,000 combatants were arrayed against 500 enemy combatants, the number of possible engagements would be proportional to the product of the two force sizes, and each engagement would be identical. Thus there is no particular advantage to the larger committed force. In modern warfare, however, concentrating the 1,000 against the enemy's 500 provides a decided advantage in that each combatant is capable of being involved in an engagement, providing essentially a two-to-one advantage to the larger committed force. Ancient warfare conforms to what is referred to as the Lanchester linear law, and modern warfare conforms to what is referred to as the Lanchester square law.[4]

Applications of Lanchester processes include both rigorous mathematical development, which assumes conflict is continuous, and simulation, which treats conflict as a series of discrete events. The mathematical approach has emphasized the use of continuous functions, particularly differential equations, though some work has been done with difference equations. The simulation approach is usually tied to discrete-time processes. The major theater-level warfare

---

[2]Taylor (1983), vol. 1.

[3]In reviewing this document, RAND colleague Paul Davis observed: "Most of the usual discussion of Lanchester equations is simply wrong. Except perhaps with circular logic or subtle footnotes, distinctions between the equations do not correspond simply to ancient versus modern warfare, to aimed versus unaimed fire, or even to the nominal ability of the sides to concentrate force—much less to a cartoon of how the combatants are lined up at an instant. The form of the aggregate attrition equations depends on a complex averaging over minibattles separated by minimaneuvers according to some set of tactics. Even qualitative features of the resulting average depend on details. For example, we might expect many so-called modern warfare battles to look in the aggregate more like linear-law battles because attrition rates will depend on either shooter-level or small-maneuver-unit search processes dependent on the density of targets. We should also expect profound asymmetries, as discussed later in the [report], and not merely because of modern information systems."

[4]There has been considerable debate on just how well these laws represent ancient and modern combat. Bracken has shown, for example, that the linear law more accurately models the Ardennes battle, a battle considered to be "modern."

simulations all have fixed time steps. Even if they draw upon data from more detailed models, say at the division level or brigade level, the underlying models typically involve fixed time steps.

In this work we take both approaches. Our initial insights were formed on the basis of adding information to time-stepped simulations. We constructed a Lanchester square simulation and a Lanchester linear simulation. In the former case, each shooter has an opportunity to detect and engage targets during each period, and this opportunity stays the same over time. In the latter case, each shooter has an opportunity to detect and engage targets during each period, but this opportunity is dependent on the number of targets.

We observed that adding possible encounters to the Lanchester square process, by hypothesizing more information, had a striking effect, as did reducing possible encounters by hypothesizing less information. We were able to demonstrate that if one side had considerable information and the other side very little, then the former followed the linear law while the latter followed the square law. We then turned to a mathematical investigation in which we developed a theory for the complete range of cases.

This chapter presents the mathematical theory and conceptual discussion first. It results in a table of all of the Lanchester laws (Table 4.1), including a number of different mixed cases. Next, the chapter presents simulation results based on varying the main parameters. These results show transitions from linear to mixed and from square to mixed. We then investigate the mixed cases in more detail.

The overall goal of this chapter is to demonstrate how adding centrally supplied information changes the dynamics of a battle and results in different tradeoffs between quality and quantity of forces.

LANCHESTER SQUARE LAW

The effect of concentrating the force is reflected by the fact that the casualty rate is assumed to depend only on the size of the shooting force. This is due to the firepower delivery available with modern weapons. If we let R and B represent the initial size of the Red and Blue forces (number of units) respectively, and N and M ($0 \leq N$, $M \leq 1$) be the effectiveness of each Red and Blue unit respectively, the rate at which each of the two forces is depleted is given by the relations

$$\frac{dr(t)}{dt} = Mb(t)$$

$$\frac{db(t)}{dt} = Nr(t),$$

where $r(t)$ and $b(t)$ represent the Red and Blue force sizes at time t and $r(0) = R$ and $b(0) = B$. The attrition to each side depends on the effectiveness of the shooting side's units and the remaining size of the shooting force. Dividing the two equations, we get

$$\frac{\dfrac{dr(t)}{dt}}{\dfrac{db(t)}{dt}} = \frac{dr(t)}{db(t)} = \frac{Mb(t)}{Nr(t)}.$$

Rearranging, we get

$$b(t)db(t) = \frac{N}{M}r(t)dr(t).$$

Integrating from time 0 to time t, we get

$$b(t)^2 - B^2 = \frac{N}{M}(r(t)^2 - R^2).$$

This formulation allows us to examine the requirements for Blue (or Red) to win. For Blue to win, we must have that at time T, $r(t) = 0$ and $b(t) > 0$. Rewriting the above equation with $t = T$ and solving for $b(T)^2$, we get

$$b(T)^2 = B^2 - \frac{N}{M}R^2 > 0.$$

Solving the inequality, we get

$$\frac{M}{N} > \left(\frac{R}{B}\right)^2.$$

For Blue to win, the relative effectiveness of the two forces must exceed the square of the initial force ratio.

One type of battle described by a Lanchester square law occurs when both sides can employ constant fractions of their forces and have target-rich environments. The size of the force the friendly commander commits to the battle determines the amount of enemy attrition attained rather than the size of the enemy force committed.

FRACTIONAL LOSS EXCHANGE RATE

We make use of the force loss exchange ratio (FLER) later in Chapter Six. It is useful to introduce it here in that it can be defined in Lanchester equation terms. The FLER is simply the ratio of Red fractional losses to Blue fractional losses, or

$$\text{FLER} = \frac{\dfrac{dr(t)}{r(t)dt}}{\dfrac{db(t)}{b(t)dt}} = \frac{dr(t)}{db(t)}\frac{b(t)}{r(t)}.$$

We can use the FLER, then, to determine who is winning. If the FLER = 1, then $dr(t)B = db(t)R$, and the sides can cause attrition to each other but are not able to improve their force ratio: it is a stalemate. If FLER > 1, Blue wins, and if FLER < 1, Red wins.

Note that for the square law,

$$\text{FLER} = \frac{dr(t)}{db(t)}\frac{b(t)}{r(t)} = \frac{M}{N}\left(\frac{b(t)}{r(t)}\right)^2.$$

At time $t = 0$, we have

$$\text{FLER} = \frac{M}{N}\left(\frac{B}{R}\right)^2.$$

Therefore, stalemate occurs when

$$\left(\frac{R}{B}\right)^2 = \frac{M}{N}.$$

To compensate for an adverse force ratio, R/B, Blue must achieve a unit effectiveness advantage equal to the square of the force ratio (M/N).

LANCHESTER LINEAR LAW

The linear law reflects the inability, or more accurately the futility, of either side to mass its forces effectively. Lanchester referred to this as a characteristic of ancient warfare:

> In olden times, when weapon directly answered weapon, the act of defence was positive and direct, the blow of sword or battleaxe was parried by sword and shield. . . . Under [these] conditions, it was not possible by any strategic plan or tactical manoeuver to bring other than equal numbers of men into the actual fighting line; one man would ordinarily find himself opposed to one man.[5]

Under these conditions, attrition depends solely upon the effectiveness of the individual combatant.

Another, more modern interpretation of the linear law is that it represents area fires. That is, we assume that the attacker knows the enemy is located within an area, but that he is unable to target each combatant individually. The best he can do is launch indirect fires into the area. In this case, the effectiveness of the attacker depends not only on the effectiveness of the weapon, but also on the number of attackers (number of weapons), the effectiveness of each attacker,

---

[5]Lanchester [1916] (1956).

and the number of targets in the area fired upon. Both of these cases result in a linear law.

As above, we let M and N be the effectiveness of each combatant, with $r(0) = R$ and $b(0) = B$, the original size of the Red and Blue forces. The number of firing opportunities for Blue is proportional to $b(t)r(t)$, and the number of Red firing opportunities is proportional to $r(t)b(t)$:[6]

$$\frac{dr(t)}{dt} = M[b(t)r(t)]$$

$$\frac{db(t)}{dt} = N[r(t)b(t)].$$

The effectiveness scores refer to the effectiveness of the individual combatant. Dividing the two equations as above, we get

$$\frac{\dfrac{dr(t)}{dt}}{\dfrac{db(t)}{dt}} = \frac{dr(t)}{db(t)} = \frac{M}{N}.$$

Rearranging, we get

$$db(t) = \frac{N}{M}dr(t).$$

Integrating from time 0 to time t, we get

$$b(t) - B = \frac{N}{M}(r(t) - R).$$

For Blue to win, we again must have that at time T, $r(T) = 0$ and $b(T) > 0$. Rewriting the above equation with $t = T$ and solving for $b(T)$, we get

---

[6]There are two ways this can come about: (1) If Blue units are searching for Red units and, when they find them, they can shoot them under target-rich conditions, then the encounter rate is proportional to the density of Red units and the kills per unit time is proportional to $r(t)b(t)$. (2) If Blue is merely firing blind, the fraction of the time it hits something is proportional to the density of Red units.

$$b(T) = B - \frac{N}{M}R > 0.$$

Solving the inequality, we get

$$\frac{M}{N} > \left(\frac{R}{B}\right).$$

In this case, to win, the effectiveness ratio need only exceed the initial force ratio. In the linear case, the impact of the force size on combat outcome is significantly less than in the square case.

The area-fires interpretation results in the following attrition rates:

$$\frac{dr(t)}{dt} = -[b(t)M]r(t)$$

$$\frac{db(t)}{dt} = [r(t)N]b(t),$$

reflecting the effects of force size, weapon effectiveness, and targets available. Here $[b(t)M]$ can be interpreted as the firing effectiveness of Blue and $[r(t)N]$ can be interpreted as the firing effectiveness of Red. Dividing the two equations as above, we get exactly the same results as above.

THE LANCHESTER MIXED LAW

We now consider adapting the Lanchester laws to account for knowledge. One approach is to consider knowledge to be a subcomponent of the unit's effectiveness score, M or N, so that $M = P(d)P(k|d)$, where $P(d)$ is the probability that a target will be detected (knowledge) and k is the effectiveness of the weapon system selected to engage the target. In this construct, we take $P(d)$ to be a measure of *local knowledge*, that is, knowledge of the enemy obtained from sources organic to the unit.

The problem is in selecting the appropriate Lanchester law. If we select the square law, we can examine the effect of an increase in Blue knowledge on Blue's ability to win. Rearranging the winning condition equation, for Blue to win, we must have that

$$\frac{B}{R} > \left(\frac{N}{M}\right)^{0.5}.$$

Let us assume that M is doubled due to an increase in Blue's knowledge. If all other variables remain the same, this has the effect of increasing the force ratio by a factor of $\sqrt{2}$ and thus enhancing the Blue win. Performing the same calculation in the linear law increases the force ratio by a factor of 2, a considerable difference. However, it is not clear which of these more closely models the effects of knowledge on combat outcomes.

As an alternative, suppose we link the *maximum possible number of encounters a unit may have in a combat cycle* to the information available to the unit from external as well as organic sources. If we let $c_r \leq b(t)$ and $c_b \leq r(t)$ represent the total number of encounters each Red unit can have with Blue units and Blue with Red respectively, then clearly $c_r = f[K_R, b(t)]$ and $c_b = g[K_B, r(t)]$. The quantities K_B and K_R represent the knowledge available to each side from external sources such as imagery from national assets, information from higher or adjacent commands, etc. These quantities are developed in Chapter Two. The cases $c_b = 1$ and $c_r = 1$ imply no external knowledge, and the sides rely on their organic sensors and sources to engage the enemy. The result is a single engagement per combat cycle. The number of encounters depends upon the information available to the unit (organic and external) and the size of the opposing force. This means that the enemy attrition rate is now dependent upon the number of units attacking, the effectiveness of the attacking unit, and the maximum number of encounters (number of targets possibly presented). This leads to the attrition that looks very much like the linear area-fires case:

$$\frac{dr(t)}{dt} = -[b(t)M]c_b$$

$$\frac{db(t)}{dt} = [r(t)N]c_r.$$

Dividing the two equations as before, we get

$$\frac{\dfrac{dr(t)}{dt}}{\dfrac{db(t)}{dt}} = \frac{dr(t)}{db(t)} = \frac{Mb(t)c_b}{Nr(t)c_r}.$$

Rearranging, we get

$$b(t)db(t) = \frac{Nc_r}{Mc_b}r(t)dr(t).$$

Integrating from time 0 to time t, we get

$$b(t)^2 - B^2 = \frac{Nc_r}{Mc_b}[r(t)^2 \quad R^2].$$

For Blue to win, we again must have that at time T, $r(T) = 0$ and $b(T) > 0$. Rewriting the above equation with $t = T$ and solving for $b(T)$, we get

$$b(T)^2 = B^2 \quad \frac{Nc_r}{Mc_b}B^2 \quad 0.$$

Solving the inequality, we get

$$\frac{Mc_b}{Nc_r} > \left(\frac{R}{B}\right)^2.$$

Although this is clearly a square law representation in this form, we can make some interesting observations by examining the nature of the Red and Blue encounters. First we observe that information has a greater effect than the effectiveness scores, in that the encounter values are not fractions, but rather numbers of units.

More interesting, however, are the results obtained by examining some extreme values for c_r and c_b. Table 4.1 summarizes the results obtained through this process. We also include an illustrative interpretation for each of the cases.

Table 4.1

Lanchester Information Laws

c_r	c_b	Condition for a Blue win	Law	Illustrative Interpretation
1	1	$\dfrac{M}{N} > \left(\dfrac{R}{B}\right)^2$	Square	Both sides rely solely on organic collection assets. No information is available from higher headquarters.
1	g	$\dfrac{Mg}{N} > \left(\dfrac{R}{B}\right)^2$	Square	In these two cases, one side has only organic collection assets and the other receives some information from higher headquarters
h	1	$\dfrac{M}{Nh} > \left(\dfrac{R}{B}\right)^2$	Square	$(0 < g < R$, and $0 < h < B)$.
B	R	$\dfrac{M}{N} > \dfrac{R}{B}$	Linear	Both sides have complete information from higher headquarters as well as information from their organic collection assets. This is the best either can do with respect to information.
B	g	$\dfrac{Mg}{N} > \dfrac{R^2}{B}$ [a]	Mixed	In these two cases, one side has knowledge of its opponent's entire force whereas the other side has only some knowledge of its opponent's force $(0 < g < R$, and $0 < h < B)$. Both sides have information available from their own organic collection assets.
h	R	$\dfrac{M}{Nh} > \dfrac{R}{B^2}$	Mixed	
B	1	$\dfrac{M}{N} > \dfrac{R^2}{B}$	Mixed	These last two cases illustrate extreme mismatches. One side receives information from higher headquarters concerning the entire enemy force whereas the other only has information from organic collection assets.
1	R	$\dfrac{M}{N} > \dfrac{R}{B^2}$	Mixed	

[a]This result was also obtained by Smith (1997) by assuming that Red attrition is proportional to the size of the Blue force, b, whereas Blue attrition is proportional to the size of both the Blue force and the Red force, mn. Thus, we get the following Lanchester differential equations: $\dfrac{db(t)}{dt} = Mr(t)b(t)$ and $\dfrac{dr(t)}{dt} = Nb(t)$. Following the usual derivation, we have that for a Blue win, we must have that $\dfrac{2M}{N} > \dfrac{R^2}{M}$. Reversing the argument produces the next case, namely $\dfrac{M}{2N} > \dfrac{R}{M^2}$.

Note that if we let $c_r = f[K_R, B] = K_R B$ and $c_b = g[K_B, R] = K_B R$, i.e., the number of encounters is directly proportional to the side's external knowledge, we get

$$\frac{\dfrac{dr(t)}{dt}}{\dfrac{db(t)}{dt}} = \frac{dr(t)}{db(t)} = \frac{Mb(t)K_B R}{Nr(t)K_R B} = \frac{Mb(t)RK_B}{Nr(t)BK_R}.$$

This is a linear model similar to the fourth case in Table 4.1. The requirement for a Blue victory then is

$$\frac{MK_B}{NK_R} > \frac{R}{B}.$$

The effect of knowledge plays a much greater role in that the force size has only linear effects. In this case, therefore, we have answered the question concerning the applicable Lanchester law.

We can also examine the effects of information dominance in this construct. Recall from Chapter Two that if, for example, Blue dominates Red, then $\delta_B \le K_B \le 1$ and $K_B > K_R$, where $0 \le \delta_B \le 1$ is the minimum knowledge required for Blue information dominance. If, at one extreme, we have that $K_B = 1.0$ and $K_R = \gamma$, where $\gamma < 1$, the requirement for a Blue victory becomes

$$\frac{M}{N\gamma} > \frac{R}{B}.$$

Even for large values of γ, it is clear that information dominance allows for a Blue victory with a less favorable (to Blue) force ratio. If both K_B and K_R are too close to γ, the effects of information dominance on winning are negligible and we have case 4 in Table 4.1.

SIMULATING THE MIXED LAW

To illustrate the effects of information on combat outcomes using the Lanchester models, we resort to a simple simulation of a stochastic process. Table 4.1 is the focus of the simulations in that we attempt to simulate conditions similar to those presented in the table. A brief description of the process is presented below.

Resources and Effectiveness Parameters

We first define a stochastic process, $\{F(t), t \in T\}$, where $F(t)$ is the force ratio of Blue to Red forces at the end of time t and T is the maximum number of time steps. Therefore, we have that the starting force ratio is $F(0) = B/R$ and, in general, $F(t) = b(t)/r(t)$, where both $b(t)$ and $r(t)$ are random variables.

Each Red and Blue unit is characterized by three effectiveness parameters: the number of targets (opposing units) each is able to encounter in a given time period, the probability that an encountered unit is detected, and the probability that a detected unit is destroyed. These last two parameters are included in the effectiveness scores, M and N above. In the stochastic process notation, we set the following:

- **Encounters.** $c_b \le r(t)$ and $c_r \le b(t)$ represent the maximum number of units a Blue and Red force can encounter during any time period respectively. As discussed above, this represents the level of knowledge available to the fighting units from sources external to the unit (usually higher headquarters) and the size of the opposing force. Although these parameters are fixed for any given simulation, a dependence on t exists because of the upper bound conditions.

- **Detections.** For these examples, we assume that local knowledge is the probability that a unit can detect a target, or $P_b(d) = d_b$ and $P_r(d) = d_r$. We further assume that these quantities are time-invariant, i.e., they are independent of the relative force sizes. This represents the knowledge available to each unit based on its organic ability to detect enemy units.

- **Attrition.** $P_b(k|d) = e_b$ and $P_r(k|d) = e_r$ are the time-invariant probabilities that Blue and Red forces are able to destroy an opponent given that a target is detected.

Therefore, force effectiveness is simply the product of these last two quantities so that $N = d_r e_r$ and $M = d_b e_b$. Recall also that $c_b = f(K_B, r(t))$ and that $c_r = g(K_R, b(t))$. That is, the number of encounters allowed depends upon the encountering side's knowledge from external sources and the size of the opposing force.

Process

The process modeled is essentially an attrition process that is modified by knowledge manifested by a restricted target set and probabilities of detection. The key to the process is determining the outcomes of the several engagements at each time period. The likelihood that a Blue/Red unit engages an opponent is based on the relative residual sizes of the forces and the values of c_b and c_r.

At each time step, the ratio $Q(t) = b(t)/[b(t) + r(t)]$ is calculated and compared to a random number, ρ, drawn from a uniform distribution defined on the interval $[0, 1]$. If $\rho \leq Q(t)$, a Blue unit has the opportunity to engage a Red unit, i.e., the Blue unit has encountered the Red target. It now remains to apply the detection probability to determine if the encountered target will be engaged. If $\rho > Q(t)$, then Red has the opportunity to engage Blue in the same way.

This continues at each time step until either the maximum allowable number of encounters on both sides have been examined or until one side or the other has no surviving units.

RESULTS FOR THE MIXED LAW

In the results that follow, we have selected force sizes and detection probabilities such that the starting force ratios are always 1.0 for varying values of c_b and c_r. In the first case, we start from the pure linear law conditions ($c_b = R$ and $c_r = B$) and then we proceed to degrade c_r, thus illustrating rows 4, 5, and 6 in Table 4.1. In the second case, we do the same for the square law case ($c_b = c_r = 1$) and cause c_r to increase, thus illustrating rows 1, 2, and 3 in Table 4.1. Finally, we treat the last two (rows 7 and 8) separately. In all cases, we treat K_B and K_R implicitly in that the functional relationships $c_b = f(K_B, r(t))$ and $c_r = f(K_R, b(t))$ are unknown.

Linear to Mixed Cases

For all the cases in this set, we assume that $e_b = e_r = 0.5$, $d_b = 0.02$, and $d_r = 0.01$. Thus, although the probability of kill given a detection is the same for both sides, Blue is twice as likely to detect a target as Red, or relative knowledge is $\Gamma = .02/.01 = 2.0$.

We begin with the pure linear case (the fourth row in Table 4.1). We first assume that both sides have access to information from sensors with a global view of the battlespace. This might be from unmanned aerial vehicles (UAVs), JSTARS satellite imagery (and the Red equivalent), or perhaps a combination of all. The implications are that this type of coverage provides external information about the location of the entire enemy force, or $c_b = R = 200$ and $c_r = B = 100$. We can easily verify that under these conditions, the outcome should result in a draw, i.e., we should have that $Nr(t) = Mb(t)$. Indeed, at time $t = 0$ we get

$$Nr(0) = d_r e_r c_b = (.01)(0.5)(200) = Mb(0) = d_b e_b c_r = (.02)(0.5)(100) = 1.0.$$

In addition, the beginning force ratio is $F(0) = 100/200 = 0.5$.

A total of 5 cycles ($T = 5$) were evaluated 100 times. The resulting average force sizes at the end of cycle 5 are $r(5) = 27.13$, and $b(5) = 14.17$. Thus we get $Mb(5) = 0.142$, and $Nr(5) = 0.136$. So we conclude that the equality condition holds approximately for this case. The final average force ratio is $F(5) = 14.17/27.13 = 0.522$.

We now examine the effect on the ending ($T = 5$) force ratio when the information available to Red from external sources deteriorates, that is, we assume that its nonorganic sensor coverage deteriorates. We also assume that both sides' organic sensors are the same as before. That is, their ability to detect and kill a target remains constant. In addition, we assume that the external information available to Red remains fixed for all 5 cycles, i.e., c_r remains fixed. Whenever $c_r \geq b(t)$, we allow the number of encounters per cycle to increase to $c_r/b(t)$ Table 4.2 lists the results of 5 cases in which we allow the number of Red encounters to decrease from $c_r = B = 100$ to $c_r = 20$. The number of Blue encounters remains fixed at $c_b = R = 200$, i.e., Blue continues to enjoy global coverage of the AO.

The data illustrate how decreasing external information affects the ending force ratio. When the Red commander receives information on the location of between 40 and 50 Blue units, the advantage swings dramatically in favor of Blue. Clearly, Blue achieves information superiority between these points, and at $c_r = 20$ it might be argued that Blue achieved information dominance.

Table 4.2

Linear to Mixed Cases

c_r	$b(5)$	$r(5)$	$F(5) = b(5)/r(5)$
100	14.17	27.13	0.522
80	14.40	27.88	0.517
60	17.76	22.22	0.799
40	31.18	12.87	2.423
20	68.21	3.92	17.401

Figure 4.1 compares the ending force sizes as fractions of the initial force sizes. The c_r values are plotted along the horizontal axis, and the fraction of the force remaining at the end of the 5 combat cycles is plotted along the vertical axis. The figure illustrates the deteriorating effect of reduced external knowledge on Red's survivability. Beyond 80 encounters per cycle, the gap between Blue and Red survivability widens rapidly, as illustrated by the sharply rising Blue curve and the rapidly declining Red curve.

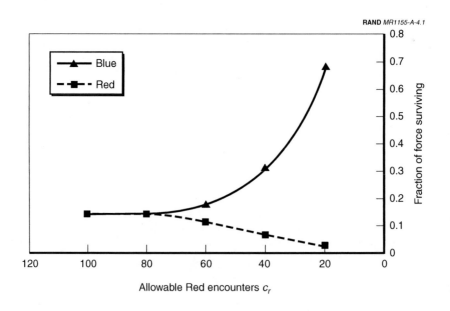

RAND MR1155-A-4.1

Figure 4.1—Ending Force Levels (Linear to Mixed)

Square to Mixed Cases

As with the linear to mixed cases, we assume that $e_b = e_r = 0.5$. However, we change the relative knowledge by increasing the Blue detection probability to $d_b = 0.08$ and the Red detection probability to $d_r = 0.02$. Now, relative knowledge is $\Gamma = .08/.02 = 4.0$. As in the previous case, Blue has local information superiority. However, this time his advantage has doubled. We begin with the pure square case (row 1 in Table 4.1). As in the previous case, if we assume that both Red and Blue have information on the location of all enemy units in the AO so that $c_b = R = 200$ and $c_r = B = 100$, we can verify that this describes a case in which the two sides fight to a draw, or $N[r(t)]^2 = M[b(t)]^2$:

$$N[r(0)]^2 = (.02)(0.5)(200)^2 = M[b(0)]^2 \quad (.08)(0.5)(100)^2 \quad 400.0 .$$

The beginning force ratio is still $F(0) = 100/200 = 0.5$.

We again evaluate a total of 5 cycles ($T = 5$) 100 times for each variant. This time however, we incrementally increase Blue's information from external sources from $c_b = 1$ to $c_b = 10$, at the same time holding Red's external information to $c_r = 1$. For the first case, in which each side receives essentially no information from external sources, the average force sizes at the end of cycle 5 are $r(5) = 180.62$ and $b(5) = 90.27$. Thus we get $M[b(5)]^2 = 324$ and $N[r(5)]^2 = 324$. Therefore, this also leads to a draw. The final average force ratio is $F(5) = 90.27/180.62 = 0.500$.

We now examine the effect on the ending ($T = 5$) force ratio when the information available to Blue from external sources improves. As above, we assume that both sides' ability to detect and kill a target remains constant. We further assume that although Blue's information from external sources increases, Red's remains at the same low level. Table 4.3 lists the results.

As the number of allowable Blue encounters increases from 1 to 10, there is a linear decrease in the Red ending force levels, while the ending Blue force levels remain approximately the same. What is interesting about these cases is the fact that the dramatic decrease in the ending Red force size was caused by only modest increases in the number of allowable Blue encounters. The major effect appears to

Table 4.3

Square to Mixed Cases

c_b	$b(5)$	$r(5)$	$F(5) = b(5)/r(5)$
1	90.27	180.6	0.500
2	90.58	161.5	0.561
3	90.94	141.2	0.644
4	91.18	122.4	0.745
5	91.97	102.1	0.901
6	92.23	82.7	1.116
7	92.74	61.8	1.500
8	92.95	44.7	2.079
9	93.05	26.4	3.529
10	93.44	11.2	8.365

be attributable to Red's inability to "know" the location of more than one enemy target at each combat cycle.

In Figure 4.2 we plot the varying levels of Blue external information along the horizontal axis. The vertical axis is the fraction of Blue and

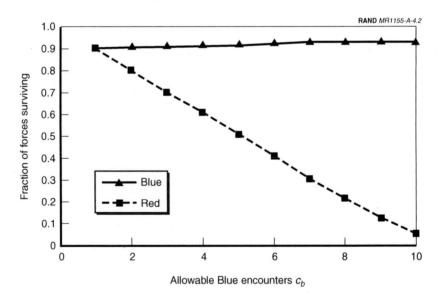

Figure 4.2—Ending Force Levels (Square to Mixed)

Red forces remaining after 5 cycles of combat. When both sides have minimal information from outside sources, they fight to a draw with 90 percent of their forces surviving. But as Blue sensor coverage increases even slightly, the fraction of Red's force surviving drops off precipitously at the rate of 10 percent for each unit of increase in c_b. The fraction of Blue's force surviving, however, remains rather constant at near 90 percent.

Pure Mixed Cases

As the base case set of assumptions for examining the pure mixed cases, we assume a greatly outnumbered Blue force with a starting size of 20 against a starting Red force of 400. We further assume that both sides have equal organic knowledge with detection probabilities of $d_b = d_r = .04$, and that the probabilities of kill given detection are $e_b = e_r = .25$. This implies that relative knowledge is $\Gamma = 1.0$, with a beginning force ratio of $F(0) = b(0)/r(0) = 0.5$. Next, we assume that Blue has extensive sensor coverage so that it knows the location of all 400 enemy units and that Red has little or no knowledge about the location of Blue forces, so that $c_b = 400$ and $c_r = 1$. This reflects the conditions described in row 8 of Table 4.1. These assumptions are similar to those proposed by Deitchman (1962) in describing guerrilla warfare such as the United States encountered in Vietnam. Only here, we credit Blue with being the small, well-hidden force with superior information from local networks.

We can verify as before that these assumptions result in a draw, $Nr(t) = M[b(t)]^2$:

$$Nr(0) = d_r e_r r(0) = (.04)(.25)(400) = 4,$$

and

$$M[b(0)]^2 = d_b e_b [b(0)]^2 = (.04)(.25)(20)^2 = 4.$$

Unlike the previous two cases, we examined two runs of 100 observations each for 5 cycles (time periods) of warfare. Table 4.4 records the surviving force sizes for both runs and the resulting average force ratios. The fact that the final force ratios for the two runs are approximately the same as the initial force ratio of 0.05, at the .05 confidence level, confirms the pure mixed law for this case.

Table 4.4

Pure Mixed Case (Base)

Run	$b(5)$	$r(5)$	$F(5) = b(5)/r(5)$
1	6.41	138.7	0.046
2	6.96	126.9	0.055

Next we examine the robustness of these findings across several cases in which the initial conditions are varied.

MIXED LAW SENSITIVITY

We now investigate the sensitivity of variations in local and external knowledge on ending force ratios for the mixed law.

Sensitivity to Local Knowledge

We first examine the sensitivity of these results to variations in knowledge as expressed by the detection probabilities. We continue to assume that both sides have equal knowledge, but at different levels. First we let the probability of detection be set to $d_b = d_r = .01$, below the 0.04 level in the previous case. Next we set it to $d_b = d_r = .10$, above the previous setting. Results for two runs of 100 observations each for the two variations are summarized in Table 4.5.

Although casualties on both sides increase considerably when their local knowledge increases, we note that for the higher detection

Table 4.5

Pure Mixed Case (Knowledge Variant)

Variant	Run	$b(5)$	$r(5)$	$F(5) = b(5)/r(5)$
$d_b = d_r = .01$	1	15.67	309.7	0.051
	2	15.54	310.7	0.050
$d_b = d_r = .10$	1	2.73	64.87	0.042
	2	3.19	57.25	0.056

probability (.10), the ratios are a bit more volatile. In all cases, however, the ending force ratio can be considered equivalent to the beginning force ratios at the .05 level of confidence.

Sensitivity to Blue External Knowledge

We now examine the effect on the surviving forces and the force ratios at $t = 0$ when the information available to Blue from higher headquarters deteriorates, i.e., as c_b decreases from 400 (the initial size of the Red force) to 300. We assume that the probabilities of both sides to detect and to kill given detection remain as in the base case above. In addition, we let the Red external information remain negligible at one encounter per cycle or $c_r = 1$. Table 4.6 and Figure 4.3 summarize the results of 100 repetitions at each encounter level.

The data illustrate the effect on the ending force ratio of decreasing the information available to Blue from external sources. There is a steady decline in the force ratio at the end of 5 periods and a steady increase in the number of surviving Red forces. In Figure 4.3, the deteriorating effects of reduced information on the location of enemy units is reflected in the number of Blue encounters per cycle. The vertical axis again records the fraction of each force surviving at the end of 5 cycles of combat. The graph depicts the rapid divergence of end strengths as Blue loses visibility over the battlespace.

Table 4.6

Pure Mixed Case (Variations in Blue External Knowledge)

c_b	$b(5)$	$r(5)$	$F(5) = b(5)/r(5)$
400	6.41	138.8	0.046
380	6.62	143.1	0.046
360	6.00	157.4	0.038
340	5.78	175.9	0.033
320	5.61	187.3	0.030
300	4.72	207.6	0.023

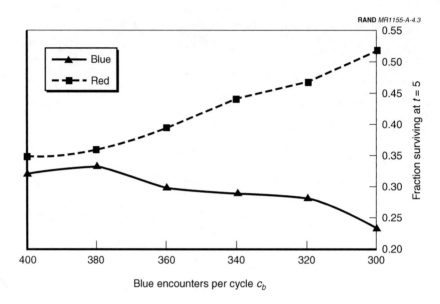

Figure 4.3—Ending Force Levels (Pure Mixed)

Sensitivity to Red External Knowledge

The mixed law as reflected in row 8 of Table 4.1 is dependent on single Red encounters. This models the case in which Red receives no information from higher headquarters and must rely solely on local knowledge to locate targets. In the previous case, we demonstrated a gradual deterioration in force ratio caused by a gradual reduction in the number of Blue encounters. However, this gradual response is not the case when the number of Red encounters is allowed to increase—even by one. That is, we observe dramatic results when the Red commander is able to receive external information that allows for even two encounters per cycle. The results listed in Table 4.7 suggest that it is critical for the Blue commander to prevent Red from receiving external information of any kind. In both cases, Blue encounters are set to 400 ($c_b = 400$).

Variance

It is of interest to observe how the variation in ending force sizes changes as parameters change. From the experimentation conducted, it appears that the outcome variance is quite sensitive to the probability of detection. For the base case with $d_b = d_r = .04$, and the variant $d_b = d_r = .10$, we conducted two sets of runs and calculated the standard deviation of the ending force sizes. The results are in Table 4.8.

Note that the dispersion in the samples is much greater for the larger detection probabilities. For example, for the .04 detection probability case, the standard deviation is approximately 60 percent of the mean Blue force size and 40 percent of the mean Red force size. In contrast, for the .10 detection probability case, the percentages vary from 105 to 136 percent of the mean ending force sizes. As local knowledge increases, it appears that the increase in attrition levels is accompanied by an increased uncertainty in the actual results.

Table 4.7

Pure Mixed Case (Variations in Red External Knowledge)

c_r	$b(5)$	$r(5)$	$F(5) = b(5)/r(5)$
1	6.41	138.7	0.046
2	0.18	239.0	0.001

Table 4.8

Pure Mixed Case (Base Case: Variance Comparisons)

Variant	Run	$b(5)$	$\sigma_{b(5)}$	$r(5)$	$\sigma_{r(5)}$
$d_b = d_r = .04$	1	6.41	3.60	138.7	53.8
	2	6.96	3.82	126.9	55.3
$d_b = d_r = .01$	1	3.79	3.98	52.47	71.45
	2	3.37	4.11	50.10	61.06

Implications

The pure mixed case illustrates how important it is to consider asymmetries in combat. Both Deitchman (1962) and Smith (1997) considered something like the mixed laws we present here, but for different reasons. In general, it challenges the basic assumptions about symmetry that generally accompany discussions about representing combat using the Lanchester models. In this discussion, we have shown how the Lanchester equations can be used to illustrate how the asymmetries associated with access to information can translate to combat advantage for the side possessing information superiority.

Before we leave this subject, it is important to make clear that we are not advocating the use of Lanchester equations to model Information-Age combat. We take the same view as our RAND colleague, Paul Davis, that the proper tools for combat analysis are simulations. Lanchester equations aggregate several combat effects into a single, constant coefficient: effects such as changes in combat posture, decisions to avoid combat, maneuvering, etc. More importantly, they do not account for the fact that these effects may vary over time.[7] In a sense, Lanchester models can be thought of as textbook representations of combat. They are useful for explaining basic principles such as we have done here, but for serious analysis of complex issues, combat simulations should be used. Davis, Blumenthal, and Gaver (1997) make just this point:

> Despite the hundreds of papers written about them, Lanchester equations (as most people understand this term) are largely irrelevant to today's combat modeling by DOD, which uses computer simulation, not simplistic constant-coefficient differential equations such as the Lanchester square law. *Lanchester equations will probably remain quite useful for making particular points in the classroom . . . or theoretical papers, but to argue about their more general validity is to chase red herrings. It is the simulations, not the Lanchester equations that should be examined* (p. 226, emphasis added.)

---

[7]In some simulations, a Lanchester-like expression is used locally, but the coefficients are adjusted in each time step. In other cases, the local algorithm is not Lanchesterian at all.

Chapter Five

TRANSITIONING TO THE INFORMATION AGE

One implication of future information superiority is a new set of concepts for all the military services. The concepts in *Joint Vision 2010*—dominant maneuver, precision engagement, full-dimensional protection, and focused logistics—are viewed as "transformations" of more traditional functions (maneuver, strike, protection, and logistics) "so powerful that they become, in effect, new concepts."

- **From maneuver to dominant maneuver.** The amount of battlespace, as well as territory, that a unit of given size will be able to control, plus the ability to deploy Army forces both strategically and operationally.

- **From strike to precision engagement.** The ability of a unit to employ its weapons precisely.

- **From protection to full-dimensional protection.** A key requirement for all military operations due to global trends toward more accurate and lethal weapons. A premium is placed on the ability to protect forces from mobilization to employment in the AO.

- **From logistics to focused logistics.** The ability to maintain a force conducting operations. Modern information systems have the potential to dramatically improve the efficiency of military logistics.

These concepts depend upon information, i.e., on the U.S. military acquiring mastery of the new technologies available in the 21st century for improved command, control, and intelligence. These technologies are presumed to yield information superiority and a "revolution in military affairs" is supposed to be the ultimate product of such transformations.

For each of the four operational concepts, we will be asking two basic questions. First, how can we best measure its effectiveness in the future; what specific MOEs are required? Second, what is the relevance of each concept to information, and vice versa? How much does the concept owe to information (e.g., "knowledge" in the parlance of the AAN) as opposed to some other variable (e.g., "speed" in AAN terms)?

THE CHANGING BATTLEFIELD

From 1914 to roughly the present day, a fundamental MOE for ground units has been their ability to control the movement of the front line of troops (FLOT) by maneuver and attrition. On the defensive, for example, an army's objective is to limit the enemy's advance. The MOE in this case is the extent to which the army can achieve the objective; it is typically measured in terms of the number of miles or kilometers by which the FLOT shifts. On the offensive, the army's goal is generally to move rapidly toward key objectives, with the MOE being the extent of FLOT forward movement (again measured in miles or kilometers) during the army's advance.

By the early 20th century, armies were of such size that continuous, "solid" fronts were feasible. These fronts could be anchored on major terrain features such as the sea and impassable mountain ranges that precluded attacks on their flanks. In addition to being feasible, these large fronts were essential because an increasingly mobile enemy could quickly exploit an open flank with reserve forces, and information about the location and intent of those reserves was generally imprecise or not available. Often, strategic or political considerations also argued for continuous fronts, as in West Germany during the Cold War. Success was measured by the ability to manage FLOT movement, which was generally represented for analytical purposes in linear fashion, as depicted by the three units lined up on the left in Figure 5.1.

In the future—as information technologies become embedded in military forces, as these forces become even more mobile, as the range and precision of their weapons increase, and as the size of

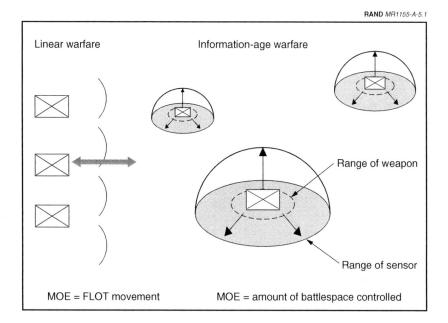

RAND *MR1155-A-5.1*

Figure 5.1—Changing MOEs

many force structures declines—success promises to be measured more in terms of the amount of battlespace a unit can *control*[1] than by FLOT movement. Battlespace control will be a function of the *speed* of the unit, its *sensors,* and its *weapons.* In many cases the range of a unit's sensors will greatly exceed the range of its weapons. This will be especially true as units farther down the chain of command gain the ability to access theater and national-level intelligence data (*external sources* in the language of Chapter Four). Thus, a unit's ability to control a battlespace will normally be measured by its weapons' ranges and unit mobility, with the sensors providing targeting, tracking, and directional information for both.

---

[1]By control, we mean in the sense of Definition 1 in Chapter Two.

BATTLESPACE CONTROL

In the future, therefore, if battlefield conditions change as a result of information technologies and move in directions indicated above, a key MOE for ground forces could become the amount of battlespace they are capable of controlling within a given theater of operations. Increasingly, this battlespace might be measured in multiple dimensions, as units seek both to employ UAVs, helicopters, and long-range rockets and missiles within their battlespaces—while denying an enemy the ability to employ similar systems—and to maneuver those battlespaces rapidly throughout the theater in pursuit of broader area control. If such changes in battlefield conditions actually come to pass in the Information Age, then analytical representations of battlespace control seem more likely to be curvilinear than linear, as in the depiction on the right side of Figure 5.1. Moreover, success might come to be measured by volumes encompassed rather than mileposts reached.

In the future, according to *Joint Vision 2020*, U.S. forces will strive to mass weapon effects rapidly rather than mass sheer numbers of forces to accomplish their missions. The large-scale introduction of 21st-century information systems is supposed to help achieve this objective. For centuries military commanders have fought in a "fog of war," which left them with imperfect knowledge of the location and status of their own forces, much less precise information about their enemy. By providing a higher-quality picture of the battlefield than ever before, *Joint Vision 2020* predicts, information will enable commanders to make decisions under conditions of considerably reduced uncertainty.

In the past, for example, the "fog of war" forced commanders to be more conservative and keep forces in reserve—in part, to hedge against lack of information. Reserves helped counter the consequences of decisions based on potentially inaccurate information. Commanders also hedged against uncertainty by waiting. They delayed action to acquire more or higher-quality information and thereby reduce the uncertainty facing them.

Although higher-quality information will not eliminate the "fog of war" or a continuing need for at least some reserves, the great reduction in overall uncertainty that information superiority is supposed to provide could force a fundamental shift in the methods used for fighting battles. Quality information should promote earlier decisive action by commanders. Increased situational or "battlespace" awareness could facilitate higher operational tempos and greater precision during operations. Better knowledge of the status of friendly forces, combined with unprecedented knowledge of the enemy, should enable logistical support, as well as both defensive and offensive military force, to be applied more efficiently.

Chapter Six

NEW MOEs FOR COMBAT OPERATIONS

In this chapter, we examine how traditional measures of combat operations might transition to Information-Age measures to account for the expanding role of information in combat operations. In addition to the measures, we focus on the metrics. In this way, we offer a way to quantify the measures that will allow for objective comparisons of alternative strategies for combat development and operational doctrine as well as actual combat operational planning. One thing we have not done is test these metrics in high-resolution simulations. It is not clear that they will be robust in all cases. What is needed is further research and testing that will undoubtedly lead to refinements to the metrics suggested here.

Of the four elements of combat operations discussed in the previous chapter, we chose to focus on two: *dominant maneuver* and *full-dimensional protection*. Similar analyses might be applied to the other two as well. For the two we have examined, we discuss how knowledge affects them and how we can measure these effects mathematically. It is important to note here that although we are focusing on the transition to Information-Age metrics, in many cases what we suggest is simply a way to incorporate the effects of information in traditional metrics. The point is that information (and hence knowledge) has always been an important component of warfare, as we stated in Chapter One. The reason for emphasis now is that its role is expanding at a considerable rate.

DOMINANT MANEUVER

Table 6.1 lists the major dominant maneuver MOEs. The metrics listed are more or less self-explanatory. Deployability is measurable in terms of pieces of equipment moved from one place to another during specified units of time. Operational reach consists of the time and distance over which a force can operate at high tempo once it has arrived within a given AO. FLOT movement, a key MOE in ground warfare for nearly a century, will remain a useful measure for future ground forces, even though by 2020 and beyond there may be less of a requirement to establish a continuous, identifiable forward line of troops measurable by such linear metrics as kilometers.

Battlespace control, a new Information-Age MOE that can be expected to overshadow FLOT movement over time, should take on increasing relevance as ground units gain the technologies—e.g., networks of joint sensors and command and control systems—that promise to give them enhanced situational awareness. This, in turn, should enable future Army units to dominate large areas without maintaining physical contact with each other to the extent that armies have since World War I.

The information effects depicted in the last column describe the effects of knowledge and speed on traditional metrics as well as define a new metric (for battlespace control) not necessarily applicable to today's combat operations. A brief description of these is presented below, followed by a more detailed mathematical definition.

Table 6.1

Measuring Dominant Maneuver in Combat

MOE	Metric	Information Effects
Deployment	Items moved per unit of time	Knowledge of enemy attempts to block routes
Operational reach	Kilometers per unit of time	Knowledge of enemy resistance along routes of advance
Battlespace control	—	Size of unit control radius and speed of unit
FLOT movement	Kilometers	Knowledge of combat capability

Knowledge of enemy attempts to block routes. The amount of material deployed to a theater of operations per unit of time depends on three factors: the size and number of lift vessels used, the speed of these vessels, and the distance traveled. The last two are clearly dependent, but if we assume a fixed speed, then the distance traveled becomes critical. If the planned shortest route is blocked by enemy activity, then deploying along that route not only increases the time required to deliver the material but may also preclude it from ever being delivered. Information needed to gain knowledge of enemy attempts (or successes) to block deployment routes, therefore, has a significant effect on deployment. The objective would be to use this knowledge to select the safest route that ensures minimum losses in transit or to call upon escort forces to clear the obstruction.

Knowledge of enemy resistance along routes of advance. This is similar to the previous effect. Resistance leads to delays and quite possibly to precluding the employment of the friendly force. Timely knowledge of enemy resistance along routes of advance offers the unit commander a choice between choosing an alternative route, eliminating the resistance, and continuing along as planned.

Knowledge of combat capability. Equally important as knowledge of enemy combat capability is the friendly unit's knowledge of its own capability. In essence this means knowledge of the FLER as defined in Chapter Four. Clearly, the distance moved when opposed by an enemy depends greatly upon the relative strength of the two opponents. Unopposed movement serves as a baseline. Knowing the FLER provides an advantage over the enemy in that the friendly unit may take actions to right an unfavorable ratio and thus improve its ability to move the FLOT.

Size of unit control radius and speed of unit. The definition of unit control radius presented in Chapter Two has, as a major component, knowledge of enemy and friendly positions within the area defined by the control radius. The effect of this knowledge is to provide the friendly unit the ability to control enemy and friendly activity within the control area. Coupled with this notion of control is the speed of the unit. In addition to knowledge, the ability of the unit to move quickly to a new location effectively expands the radius of control.

METRICS FOR DOMINANT MANEUVER

The dominant maneuver MOEs for future combat are developed in parallel with three campaign phases: deployment, employment, and combat operations. The metrics defined below follow this sequence. The two attributes of the future force that figure prominently in all of the calculations are *knowledge* and *speed*. The first of these is addressed explicitly in all metrics. The second is included as a component of the metric. Within this construct, the metrics are developed with two objectives in mind: (1) to present a reasonable mathematical argument for describing the degree to which a combat phenomenon favors the friendly commander and (2) to show, through the application of knowledge to the combat metric, how information improves combat outcomes.

Deployment

The deployment metric should measure how well the friendly commander is able to move a combat force from a CONUS embarkation site to an overseas debarkation location in the AO. We assume several routes are available to move the unit as well as multiple means of delivery. We further assume that the effective speed of the convoy is known. By convoy in this context, we mean the ships, aircraft, and/or organic lift used to transport the unit.

Figure 6.1 illustrates a network of possible routes from a CONUS embarkation point to a debarkation location in the AO. The $t_{i,j}$ values on the arcs represent the unimpeded time required for the unit to travel between nodes i and j. The nodes in the network represent airfields, seaports, navigation points, or intermediate staging points (ISPs) en route to the AO.

The objective is to move the force from node 1 in CONUS to node 6 in the AO in the shortest amount of time. The MOE therefore is an integral component of the shortest route methodology encompassing time, force protection, and knowledge. Knowledge in this case allows us to select a route that better protects the force or, if risk can be tolerated, the fastest route. The metric is developed in the following sequence:

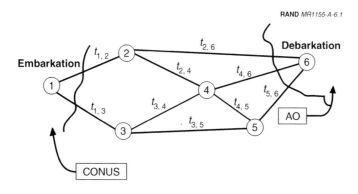

Figure 6.1—Alternate Deployment Routes

Step 1. Using standard network theory,[1] calculate the shortest (least time) unobstructed path from node 1 to node 6. The $t_{i,j}$ are calculated from knowledge of the distances between nodes, $d_{i,j}$, and the effective convoy speed, s: $t_{i,j} = \dfrac{d_{i,j}}{s}$. Suppose the shortest path is $T^* = t_{1,2} + t_{2,4} + t_{4,6}$. The quantity T^* then represents the minimum unobstructed time required to reach the in-theater point of debarkation.

Step 2. If one or more of the paths between the nodes is obstructed, then the movement of the force may not be unimpeded. Obstructions to movement such as weather, terrain, and/or enemy action may be encountered on one or more of the route segments (paths). This will have the effect of impeding travel on those segments as measured by an increase in time to travel between affected nodes. For storms and/or rough terrain, the increase in transit time derives from the reduced convoy speed. For enemy action, we would expect escort ships or aircraft to be directed to engage the enemy before the convoy is allowed to proceed. In any event, safe transit time increases on the segment.

If we have knowledge of the obstruction(s) along the transit routes, we can recalculate the shortest route from 1 to 6. The new route

---

[1]See, for example, Wagner (1969).

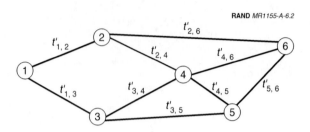

RAND *MR1155-A-6.2*

Figure 6.2—Alternate Deployment Routes with Possible Obstructions

would either avoid the obstructions or minimize the time lost from those obstructed segments that are unavoidable. The newly reconfigured route depicted in Figure 6.2 assumes that we have some intelligence that might cause us to reevaluate the network.

The quantities on the paths ($t'_{i,j}$) represent the revised estimates of the transit times based on reports of possible obstructions. Because not all of the arcs are obstructed in some way, we have that $t'_{i,j} \geq t_{i,j}$, the equality holding for unobstructed paths. By definition $t_{i,j}$ is the minimum transit time between i and j, and therefore it cannot be reduced. This information is used to calculate a revised total transit time estimate, T^*_{rev}. The problem is to assess the effect of knowledge gained from the sensor reports on the accuracy of T^*_{rev}.

Step 3. This step allows us to assess the value of information received from the sensors and, therefore, the effects of knowledge on deployment planning. In this and subsequent analyses, we quantify the knowledge in a geometric region of interest. For example, by enclosing the route maps in Figures 6.1 and 6.2 in a rectangle as depicted in Figure 6.3, the area of interest in planning the deployment is represented by the rectangular area, A.

Clearly, the friendly commander would like to have complete, unambiguous knowledge about all obstructions in the area. The amount of sensor coverage is a metric that can measure the degree to which this is known. Its development follows.

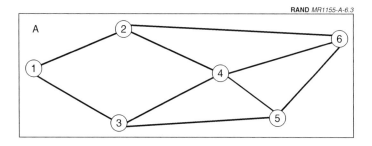

Figure 6.3—Rectangular Area of Interest

If we let S represent the area within A covered by all types of sensors (satellites, organic sensors, etc.), then three possibilities exist: $S > A$, $S = A$, or $S < A$. The ratio S/A then can be thought of as the number of possible observations of obstacles in the area, A. If $S > A$, we experience redundant coverage and the number of possible observations is greater than 1. If $S \leq A$, then we can expect 1 or fewer observations. It is also possible to experience gaps in coverage so that it is possible for S to exceed A and still experience voids in coverage. In these cases, we need to depress S so that the ratio S/A is less than 1. One way this can accommodated without resorting to the complication of identifying the actual region of coverage is to penalize for voids in coverage. For example, suppose ϕ represents the area covered by the sum of the sensor coverage and θ represents the AO. Furthermore, let $G = \|\phi \cap \theta\|$ represent the area common to both ϕ and θ. We can now modify the ratio to read $[S - (A - G)]/A$. Note that if $\phi \cap \theta = \theta$, then $G = A$, that is, there are no voids. We cannot have that $\phi \cap \theta \not\subset \varnothing$, because coverage by each sensor is assumed to be coverage within the AO. Therefore for all other cases, $G < A$. This formulation then accounts for voids in coverage without explicitly locating the void. If we let d be the probability that an obstacle will be detected, then knowledge can be represented as

$$K = 1 - (1-d)^{\frac{S-(A-G)}{A}}.$$

Note that this works equally well if there are no obstacles. It is simply a measure of the knowledge gained from the sensor suite.

Recall that the estimates in Figure 6.2 were made based on the sensor reports received. The knowledge factor, K, then should affect the accuracy of these reports and therefore the accuracy of T^*_{rev}. One way to do that is to examine the ratio

$$\frac{T^* + K\Delta}{T^* + \Delta},$$

where $\Delta = |T^*_{rev} - T^*|$ and $T^* = T^*_{rev}$. For K near 1, near-perfect knowledge, the ratio is approximately 1, indicating good information quality. For smaller values of K near 0, it becomes the ratio of the total transit time without obstacles to the revised estimate. This quantity will be small if there is indeed a large reported time delay.

Operational Reach

Once in the AO, forces must be tactically employed. This means movement from the point of debarkation to locations within the AO. The battlefield of the future is likely to be much more nonlinear than today, so units will be required to move to widely dispersed areas of the AO. We can extend the idea of named areas of interest (NAIs) to include those areas where units are to be employed. The assumption is that on the battlefield of the future, NAIs are no longer just areas forward of the friendly forces, but rather widely dispersed areas requiring the presence of friendly forces to cover enemy activity in their proximity.[2] Figure 6.4 depicts a notional deployment of this kind. Units move to employment areas where they are positioned to cover the NAIs. In this example, we depict three units designated to cover four NAIs. We revisit this concept later in assessing the speed of the units and the total volume of battlespace they are expected to control.

In moving from the debarkation point to the employment areas, alternative routes are planned in much the same way deployment routes were planned for deployments. These routes may or may not

---

[2]The methodology is not dependent upon this extended concept of an NAI. As long as the force must be employed in a widely dispersed area, the methodology applies.

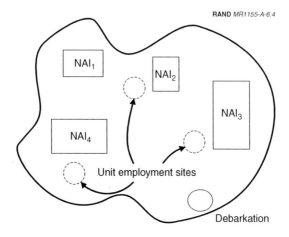

RAND *MR1155-A-6.4*

Figure 6.4—Planned Employment Areas

be obstructed (although most likely they will be) as in the deployment case. Finding the "shortest" and safest route to the employment area is still the objective of this phase of the operation. The methodologies presented for the deployment case apply here as well. Figure 6.5 illustrates a notional in-theater route network for one of the three units deployed.

The metric is the time expended in moving from the debarkation point in the AO to the employment area. As with deployment from CONUS, sensors and sources covering the geographic area enclosing all alternative routes are used to calculate the knowledge factor. The revealed obstructions on the path and the commander's willingness or need to take risks then factor into the calculation of the appropriate course of action.

Battlespace Control

The degree to which a unit controls the overall battlespace can be measured in terms of its engagement geometry and the geometry of the target NAIs. The assumption implicit in such a measure is that in the future, combat units will be deployed to widely dispersed locations in the AO to control areas deemed critical to the overall success of the campaign. We also expect that future forces will be capable of

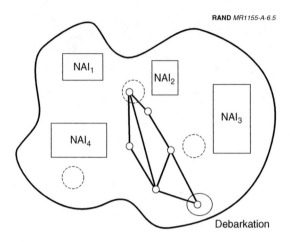

Figure 6.5—Alternate In-Theater Routes

moving faster than today's forces, thus increasing the battlespace they are able to control as a function of time as well as distance. Speed, then, is another measure of battlespace control. In developing a metric that adequately reflects the essential aspects of battlespace control in the future, both the geometry of the friendly force employment and the speed at which it is able to deploy and redeploy must be considered.

Relative geometry. The unit employment geometry is a hemisphere (Figure 5.1) with radius r_i, the unit *control radius* as defined in Chapter Two. So we can calculate the space controlled by unit i to be

$$B_i = \frac{2\pi}{3} r_i^3$$

and the total battlespace controlled by Blue to be B, the sum of the space controlled by the Blue units or

$$B \leq \frac{2\pi}{3} \sum_i r_i^3 .$$

The inequality refers to the possibility that several of the units overlap coverage.

The NAIs in the AO are generally described as rectangular areas (although they need not be). If we consider the space above the NAI as part of the battlespace, then the quantity comparable to B is $V = \sum_j V_j$, where V_j is the volume of the jth NAI. Two basic conditions exist. First, if the friendly force is too far removed from the NAI, it is not able to exercise control over it. We can describe this in terms of overlapping space, i.e., if $B \cap V = \varnothing$, then the measure of battlespace control is zero or $D = 0$. Second, if $B \cap V \neq \varnothing$, then there is some overlap between B and V, and dominance is simply the ratio of the overlap to the size of V. If B is contained in $V (B \subset V)$, then $D = \dfrac{B}{V}$. If V is contained in $B (V \subset B)$, then $D = 1$. For all other cases, $D = \dfrac{S(B \cap V)}{V}$, where $S(B \cap V)$ is the magnitude of the overlap. We now examine the contribution of speed and knowledge to D.

Speed. Beginning with speed, we develop a factor of D that reflects the degree to which the Blue units are able to move from one NAI to another and thereby increase the battlespace they control. Consider the following example. Suppose the AO consists of five NAIs as depicted in Figure 6.6. The black dot in each NAI represents the ideal location from which it can be controlled. The distance between NAI_i and NAI_j is denoted as $d_{i,j}$. If we assume that all the units in the force are positioned to cover at least one NAI, then the task is to determine the total minimum distance required to connect all the NAIs in the AO. A conservative approach is to find the sum of the branch lengths on a minimal spanning tree.[3] The left-hand graphic in Figure 6.7 records the distances between the NAIs and the right-hand graphic depicts the minimal spanning tree. The total minimum distance in this special case is $d = 22$. For simplicity, we now assume that all units travel at the same speed over all routes. We can easily relax this assumption without too much difficulty if the units involved in the force are dissimilar and therefore travel at varying speeds along the connecting routes. The time required by any of the units to travel the 22-unit distance is $\tau = d / s$, where s is the nominal speed of the friendly units in the force.

---

[3]See Ford and Fulkerson (1962).

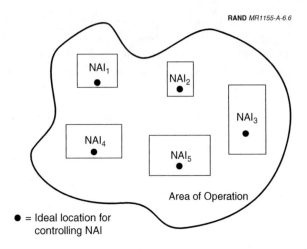

Figure 6.6—Area of Operations with Five Named Areas of Interest

The objective of this analysis is to illustrate how speed affects the ability of the force to control the battlespace.[4] We would expect that as τ gets small, i.e., as either the distances get smaller or the units can travel faster, the force's ability to cover the battlespace, and therefore improve its ability to control it, increases. Mathematically, we seek a function of τ, $g(\tau)$, that increases in value as τ decreases. One such function is $g(\tau) = e^{-a\tau}$ for $\tau \geq 0$. In this formulation, the exponential coefficient, $a > 0$, is a *shape* parameter. Its function is to model the rate at which the curve depicted in Figure 6.8 approaches zero as τ gets large. For large a, $g(\tau)$ decreases rapidly, whereas for small a, the reverse is true. In one sense, we can refer to $g(\tau)$ as an *agility* factor, i.e., a measure of the degree to which the force is capable of maneuvering between NAIs.

A rapid force will experience a large agility factor in that the time required for it to travel to all of the NAIs will be relatively small. Conversely, as the force slows down, the agility factor decreases because

---

[4]Although we do not assume that a single unit will visit all NAIs, the minimal spanning tree distance can be thought of as the minimum distance required for one unit to do so. This creates an effective upper bound on the actual distances traveled. The point here is that speed is a force divisor. That is, the further a unit must travel to get to the fight, the less effective it is.

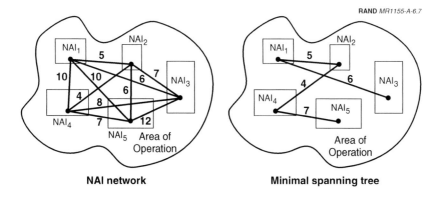

Figure 6.7—Minimum Distance to All Named Areas of Interest

of the increased time required to travel to the NAIs. Finally, we note that the factor is between 0 and 1 and can therefore be applied directly to the battlespace control metric, D, as a multiplier so that we get $D' = g(\tau)D$. Then $g(\tau)$ can be thought of as an agility force multiplier. Using the agility factor in this way highlights the fact that in the absence of $g(\tau)$, the metric D is overstated. That is, battlespace control without speed is less effective.

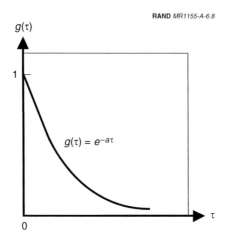

Figure 6.8—Force Agility Factor

Knowledge. We now examine the effects of knowledge on battle-space control. Recall that the knowledge metric was defined as the ratio of Blue to Red knowledge densities, or $\Gamma = K_B / K_R$, and that therefore R ⊕ . If $\Gamma < 1$, then Red has information superiority over Blue; if $\Gamma > 1$, Blue has information superiority; and if $\Gamma = 1$, both are equally competent and information is not a factor. If we apply this directly to the agility modified battlespace control metric, we get

$$D' = RD' \mp g(\tau)D.$$

For $\Gamma < 1$, the battlespace metric is reduced, indicating that Red information superiority has an adverse effect on Blue's ability to control the battlespace. For $\Gamma > 1$, the metric is increased, reflecting the value of Blue's information superiority on battlespace control. For $\Gamma = 1$, Blue and Red are equally capable, and information has no effect on battlespace control.

FLOT Movement

Some portions of future battles will probably resemble today's battles. In some cases, the best tactic for the situation facing the Blue force will be to advance along a traditional front. The fact that legacy forces will still be in the Army's inventory reinforces the likelihood that traditional FLOT movement will not be completely abandoned. The question then is, How will the future information-based force influence the movement of the FLOT in battle? This section addresses the dual problem of measuring FLOT movement using traditional, attrition-based metrics and the influence of knowledge and speed.

We begin with some basic ideas. First, we assume that there is a nominal, unopposed unit speed, f_i, associated with each unit participating in the attack (or defense). We further assume that this is the best the unit can do. That is, for any environment, this nominal speed cannot be exceeded.[5] The actual speed of the unit, a_i, is always less than or equal to f_i depending upon conditions in the AO. Clearly, if $a_i = 0$, the unit has been halted or is in a defensive position and is

---

[5]We can think of this as the unopposed speed of the slowest element in the unit.

holding. If $a_i < 0$, the unit is withdrawing. For the entire friendly force in the AO, we define $f = \min\{f_1, f_2, \ldots, f_n\}$ to be the nominal unopposed speed of the force.

Next, we consider the traditional attrition-based metric, the force loss exchange ratio (FLER). The FLER is an estimate of the relative combat power of the opposing forces and is defined as the ratio of percentage losses, or

$$\text{FLER} = F = \frac{\text{fraction of Red losses}}{\text{fraction of Blue losses}}.$$

As with relative knowledge, we have that $F > 1$ favors Blue, $0 \leq F < 1$ favors Red, and $F = 1$ reflects evenly matched forces.

As a measure of relative combat power, we would expect that the FLER has an effect on the movement of the FLOT. From the Blue perspective, a favorable FLER should increase the actual FLOT speed closer to the nominal maximum unopposed speed of the force, or

$$\lim_{F \to \infty} a = f,$$

where a is the actual opposed nominal speed of the force defined as $a = \min\{a_1, a_2, \ldots, a_n\}$. This argues for the development of an expression, $m(F)$, that reflects the slowing of Blue's forward movement or reversing its direction in Red's favor when $0 \leq F < 1$, and it reflects the effective forward movement of Blue closer to f when $F \geq 1$.[6] A function that has these properties can be constructed from the function

$$h(F) = 1 - e^{-bF}.$$

Figure 6.9 depicts this curve with the important $F = 1$ break point. As with the agility factor, a, the exponential coefficient $b > 0$ is a shaping parameter that determines the rate at which $h(F) \to 1$.

---

[6]Actually, we might envision some point at which the forces disengage due to one side facing an unfavorable FLER. Like the point at which information superiority becomes information dominance, the point of disengagement is situation dependent.

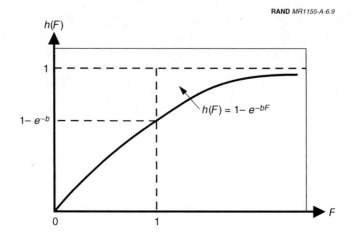

Figure 6.9—FLER Factor

Taking advantage of the properties of $h(F)$, we can now define the FLOT movement factor as follows:

$$m(F) = \begin{cases} v\,\dfrac{e^{-\frac{b}{2}} - e^{-bF}}{h(F)} & \text{for } 0 < F \leq 1 \\[2em] h(F) & \text{for } F > 1. \end{cases}$$

The factor v is used to smooth the discontinuity between both pieces of the function so that

$$v = \frac{(1 - e^{-b})^2}{e^{-\frac{b}{2}} - e^{-b}}.$$

We refer to $m(F)$ as the *effective FLOT movement* based on the relative combat strength of both sides. For $0.5 \leq F < 1$, Blue continues to advance but at a slowing rate until its forward movement stops when $F = 0.5$.[7] For smaller values of F, we have

---

[7]The selection of $F = 0.5$ as the point at which the Blue advance stops is arbitrary. It is perhaps better left as a metric parameter that can be adjusted to suit the application.

$$\lim_{F \to 0} v \frac{e^{-\frac{b}{2}} - e^{-bF}}{1 - e^{-bF}} \to \infty \quad .$$

Note that applying this factor to f could result in a "rout" speed that exceeds f. Hopefully, this case will always be uninteresting, and therefore we can ignore the possibility or conclude that if it occurs, our plans will require drastic adjustment.

For large $F \geq 1$,

$$\lim_{F \to \infty} h(F) = \lim_{F \to \infty} \left(1 - e^{-bF}\right) = 1.$$

Therefore we get that $m(F) \to f$, as desired.

The same argument can be applied to knowledge. We would expect that improved situational awareness would allow the Blue commander to choose tactics that would have the effect of moving the FLOT forward. For example, suppose the friendly commander receives reliable intelligence that the enemy is about to commit his reserves in a flanking movement designed to turn the friendly force. If the friendly commander uses this information to maneuver around the enemy and thus penetrate his rear area, he will most likely cut the enemy force from its lines of communications and, thus, effectively move the FLOT forward.

As with the previous metrics, we seek an expression, $k(\Gamma)$, that acts to increase the forward movement of the FLOT [increases $m(F)$] whenever $\Gamma > 1$, that acts to slow or reverse the forward direction of the FLOT whenever $\Gamma < 1$, and has no effect when $\Gamma = 1$.

The same functional relationship used for F can be used here, namely $k(\Gamma) = 1 - e^{-b\Gamma}$ (see Figure 6.10). Applying $k(\Gamma)$ to $m(F)$ is a bit more complex, in that the addition of Γ creates four conditions that must be examined separately.

Case 1: $0 < F \leq 1$ and $0 \leq \Gamma < 1$. This is the worst possible case for Blue. It implies an enemy superior in strength and with superior knowledge of the combat situation. The effect of diminished knowledge is to further slow the forward movement of Blue, and to hasten

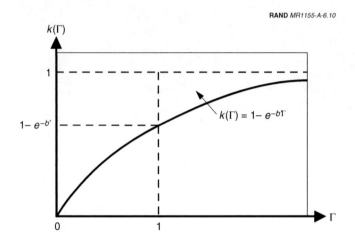

RAND *MR1155-A-6.10*

Figure 6.10—Knowledge Factor for FLOT Movement

its withdrawal. Reversing the example above, suppose Red again decides to commit its reserves to turn the Blue flank as before. Now, Red is a superior force and is aware of Blue's inferior condition. In addition, Blue is not likely to know of Red's intentions. In this case, Red is likely to be successful in either halting Blue's advance or actually forcing a Blue withdrawal.

First, even without considering the unfavorable information superiority, we have that

$$m(F) = \frac{e^{-\frac{b}{2}} - e^{-bF}}{1 - e^{-bF}} \cdot 8$$

We can model this in the metric by increasing the term e^{-bF} in the numerator for decreasing Γ. This can be accomplished as follows:

---

[8]We drop the smoothing factor here, recognizing that by doing so we may introduce discontinuities in the function. In those cases where the discontinuities are counter-intuitive, a smoothing factor should be added.

$$M(F,\Gamma) = \frac{e^{-\frac{b}{2}} - e^{-bF} / k(\Gamma)}{1 - e^{-bF}}.$$

For the full range of Γ, the second term in the numerator exceeds e^{-bF}. We have therefore that

$$\lim_{\Gamma \to 0} M(F,\Gamma) = \infty \quad \text{and} \quad \lim_{\Gamma \to 1} M(F,\Gamma) = \frac{e^{-\frac{b}{2}} - e^{-bF} / (1 - e^{-b'})}{1 - e^{-bF}}.$$

Case 2: $0 \le F < 1$ and $\Gamma \ge 1$. In this case, it is possible that Blue's superior knowledge could mitigate its combat deficiency. Continuing with the previous example, the situation for Blue is not as desperate. The Red commander, as before, wishes to turn the Blue flank by committing his reserves. But in this case, Blue is able to detect Red's maneuver early enough to maneuver to avoid contact with his weakened force. This may not move the FLOT forward, but it will slow a possible Blue withdrawal.

As in Case 1, the FLER factor alone is

$$m(F) = \frac{e^{-\frac{b}{2}} - e^{-bF}}{1 - e^{-bF}}.$$

In this case, however, we can model the positive effects of information superiority by allowing the first term in the numerator to increase with increasing Γ. The following expression does this:

$$M(F,\Gamma) = \frac{e^{-\frac{b}{2}} / (1 - k(\Gamma)) - e^{-bF}}{1 - e^{-bF}}.$$

For all values of $\Gamma \ge 1$, the first term in the numerator is greater than $e^{-\frac{b}{2}}$. Examining the limits, we have

$$\lim_{\Gamma \to \infty} M(F,\Gamma) = \infty \quad \text{and} \quad \lim_{\Gamma \to 1} M(F,\Gamma) = \frac{e^{-\frac{b}{2}}/e^{-b'} - e^{-bF}}{1 - e^{-bF}}.$$

Clearly, the first limit exceeds 1, and it is possible that the second also exceeds 1. Therefore we must have that

$$M(F,\Gamma) = \min\left[\frac{e^{-\frac{b}{2}}/(1 - k(\Gamma)) - e^{-bF}}{1 - e^{-bF}}, 1 \right].$$

Of interest in this case is the possibility for information superiority to compensate for combat deficiency, as illustrated in the next example.

Case 3: $F \geq 1$ and $0 \leq \Gamma < 1$. This case reverses Case 2. That is, here we would expect the lack of information superiority to reduce the effect of superior combat power. Now, the commander of the inferior Red force uses his superior knowledge of the combat situation to accurately locate Blue's vulnerable flank and commits his reserves to effectively turn the Blue force. Blue on the other hand, is unable to detect Red's plan until it is too late to maneuver effectively. This is reminiscent of the Mongol tactics described in Chapter Two.

In this case, the FLER factor is $m(F) = 1 - e^{-bF}$. Lack of information superiority has the effect of reducing this factor. The following metric accomplishes this: $M(F, \Gamma) = (1 - e^{-bF})k(\Gamma)$. In this case the limits on Γ produce the following:

$$\lim_{\Gamma \to 0} M(F,\Gamma) = 0 \quad \text{and} \quad \lim_{\Gamma \to 1} M(F,\Gamma) = (1 - e^{-bF})(1 - e^{-b'}).$$

Notice that the worst case, $(\Gamma = 0)$, has the effect of stopping Blue's forward progress. The metric does not model a Blue withdrawal. The rationale is that even without information superiority, Blue's superior combat power would, at worst, result in Blue's assuming a defensive position.

Case 4: $F \geq 1$ and $\Gamma \geq 1$. This is the best case for Blue. It enjoys both combat superiority and information superiority. Red's desperate attempt to turn Blue's flank is now discerned by a superior Blue in enough time for the Blue commander either to maneuver his forces to get behind the advancing Red force, or to meet him with his superior force. In each case, the FLOT is likely to move in favor of the Blue force.

Beginning with the FLER factor as in Case 3, $m(F) = 1 - e^{-bF}$, we would expect information superiority to act as a force multiplier, thus increasing $m(F)$. This is accomplished with the metric

$$M(F,\Gamma) = \frac{1 - e^{-bF}}{1 - k(\Gamma)}.$$

The limits on Γ produce the following results:

$$\lim_{\Gamma \to \infty} M(F,\Gamma) = \infty \quad \text{and} \quad \lim_{\Gamma \to 1} M(F,\Gamma) = \frac{1 - e^{-bF}}{e^{-b'}}.$$

As in Case 2, we must restrict the factor to 1, and therefore

$$M(F,\Gamma) = \min\left[\frac{1 - e^{-bF}}{e^{-b'T}}, 1 \right].$$

These four cases attempt to represent the full range of relative strength and relative knowledge effects on FLOT movement. They attempt to answer our original question: How will the future information-based force influence the movement of the FLOT in battle? The degree to which they accurately reflect the true effects remains to be seen. What can be said, however, is that they suggest a likely approach to modeling these effects. Figure 6.11 summarizes the discussion.

MEASURES FOR FULL-DIMENSIONAL PROTECTION

Table 6.2 lists the major MOEs for full-dimensional protection. Of the three measures listed, the degree to which a unit is capable of protecting itself from fires gains the most from the transition from traditional to Information-Age metrics. The reason is that informa-

RAND *MR1155-A-6.11*

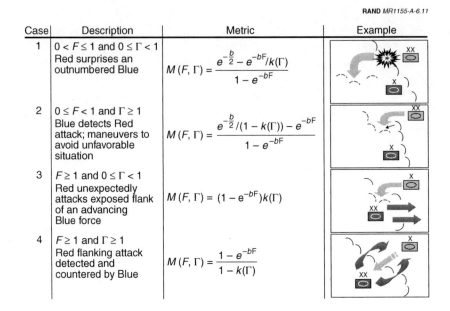

Case	Description	Metric	Example
1	$0 < F \le 1$ and $0 \le \Gamma < 1$ Red surprises an outnumbered Blue	$M(F, \Gamma) = \dfrac{e^{-\frac{b}{2}} - e^{-bF}/k(\Gamma)}{1 - e^{-bF}}$	
2	$0 \le F < 1$ and $\Gamma \ge 1$ Blue detects Red attack; maneuvers to avoid unfavorable situation	$M(F, \Gamma) = \dfrac{e^{-\frac{b}{2}}/(1 - k(\Gamma)) - e^{-bF}}{1 - e^{-bF}}$	
3	$F \ge 1$ and $0 \le \Gamma < 1$ Red unexpectedly attacks exposed flank of an advancing Blue force	$M(F, \Gamma) = (1 - e^{-bF})k(\Gamma)$	
4	$F \ge 1$ and $\Gamma \ge 1$ Red flanking attack detected and countered by Blue	$M(F, \Gamma) = \dfrac{1 - e^{-bF}}{1 - k(\Gamma)}$	

Figure 6.11—Effects of Knowledge on FLOT Movement

tion has a dominant role in all three components of the metric. In the future, we can expect an enemy to have sophisticated sensor systems and more accurate direct-fire and indirect-fire weapons capable of threatening friendly forces anywhere in the AO. We can also expect an increase in the amount and capability of enemy IW systems. Full-dimensional protection then encompasses both physical protection and protection against hostile electronic intrusion. Consequently, we focus on hardness (protection by physical means), deception (protection by illusion), and mobility (protection by evasion).

The Information-Age metrics depicted in the last column reflect the effects of knowledge and speed on traditional protection metrics. The number of combat losses will continue to be the casualty metric, but we would expect the number to decrease with effective protection measures.

Table 6.2

Measuring Full-Dimensional Protection in Combat

MOE	Traditional Metric	Information-Age Metric
Protection from direct and indirect fires	Hardness, deception, and mobility	Knowledge-enhanced hardness, deception, and mobility
Casualties	Number of losses	Number of losses

Hardness

Hardness measures the degree to which a unit can withstand physical or electronic attack. For example, troop and equipment shelters provide protection against overpressure, vehicle armor provides protection against penetration, and shielding protects electronic equipment against high-altitude EMP bursts. We can use standard metrics for each of these, such as pounds per square inch (PSI) for overpressure, inches of armor for penetration, and volts per meter for EMP.

In this work, we focus on overpressure. The reason is that at the operational level, armor protection and EMP shielding are generally fixed. That is, the unit commander most likely will not have much flexibility in altering the levels of either—even on the future battlefield.

The effectiveness of hardening is based on the Blue commander's ability to know what type of weapon the enemy intends to use against him and where the attack will occur. From the enemy's perspective, the Red commander may defeat the Blue defenses if he can detect the Blue commander's plan. This allows the Red commander to select the appropriate weapons and to direct his attack against protected areas or attack before adequate defenses are completed. These ideas are quantified in the hardness metric defined next.

We begin with a measure of physical *hardness sufficiency*, i.e., the degree to which a shelter or shield is hard enough to protect the force. A simple metric that expresses this notion is

$$H = \frac{P_B}{P_R},$$

where P_B is the equivalent overpressure in PSI of any shelter used to protect equipment and troops, and P_R is the overpressure created by the enemy weapon used in an attack on the shelter. If $H > 1$, the shelter is "overdesigned"; if $H = 1$, it is adequate to protect the force against the enemy weapon; and if $H < 1$, the shelter is inadequate. Ideally, we would like $H = 1$. That is, we expend just the right amount of time and resources in constructing the shelter. If we err, however, we would rather that $H > 1$.

The Blue commander's goal is to achieve $H = 1$ by gathering intelligence on Red's weapon systems and possible approach routes. We assume that the Blue commander has the means at his disposal to control P_B, i.e., that Blue can always construct an adequate shelter. All he needs is information about P_R. In the absence of good intelligence, we would prefer that $H > 1$.

If $\Gamma < 1$, Red has an information advantage, and we assume that it would be in the Red commander's interest to use his superior knowledge to ensure that $H < 1$. If $\Gamma \geq 1$, then Blue's knowledge is at least as good as Red's, and the Blue commander would most likely use his advantage to ensure that H is as close to 1 as possible. In any event, the Blue commander would never allow H to drop below 1. A simple metric that reflects these conditions is

$$H_\Gamma = \begin{cases} \Gamma \text{ if } 0 \leq \Gamma < 1 \\ 1 + \frac{1}{\Gamma} \text{ if } \Gamma \geq 1. \end{cases}$$

H_Γ is relative hardness with knowledge. If Red enjoys information superiority ($\Gamma < 1$), then H_Γ is always less than 1. But if Blue has equal or superior knowledge ($\Gamma \geq 1$), then as $\Gamma \to \infty$, i.e., as Blue's information superiority improves, $H_\Gamma \to 1$ and the Blue commander is able to adequately harden against an enemy attack. As the lower level, where the Blue commander's knowledge is only marginally superior, $H_\Gamma \to 2$. That is, as he approaches information parity with Red, relative knowledge decreases and the Blue commander tends to overdesign.

Deception

Deception consists of all forms of illusion, from physical decoys to electronic signature spoofing. It is any act that attempts to make the enemy commander believe a false premise about the friendly force or his own forces. In this sense, it encompasses information operations concerned with inserting false information in the enemy's information systems. Cover and concealment are also components of deception, in that they deny the enemy information on the location of friendly forces.

Intelligence plays a major role in deception. Deception is thwarted by superior knowledge. It is only possible to deceive if the enemy cannot know the true relative disposition of Blue and Red forces. However, the enemy must have sufficient relative capability to detect the erroneous picture as true.

If, as before, we assume that the Blue commander has the means to initiate deception measures of all kinds, then the relative knowledge, Γ, can be used directly as a deception metric. If $\Gamma < 1$, then Red has superior knowledge, and Blue attempts at deception are likely to fail. As Blue gains in relative knowledge, i.e., as $\mapsto$, the likelihood that Blue will be successful at deception increases. This suggests a probability-of-success metric based on relative knowledge. If we let $P(\delta\,|\,\Gamma)$ $f(\Gamma)$ be the probability that Blue deception activities (δ) will be successful conditioned on relative knowledge, then $f(\Gamma) = 1 - 2^{-\Gamma}$ has the desired characteristics (see Figure 6.12).

In the region where Red has information dominance, i.e., where $\Gamma < 1$, Blue's probability of success is less than 0.5 ($P(\delta\,|\,\Gamma) < 0.5$). When $\Gamma = 0$, the probability drops to 0, indicating that it is impossible to conduct deception operations in the absence of any intelligence capability. With information parity, the probability of success is even, i.e., $P(\delta\,|\,\Gamma)$ 0.5, and as Blue gains in information superiority, ($\mapsto$), $P(\delta\,|\,\Gamma) \rightarrow 1$.

Mobility

Mobility as a force protection measure describes a unit's ability to relocate from its current (perhaps exposed) position to a safe location. In this sense, it can be considered a measure of the unit's

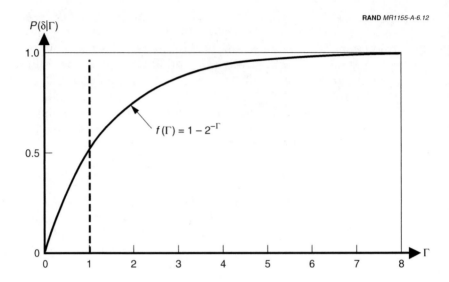

Figure 6.12—Probability of Successful Deception

agility. The objective is to avoid destruction by evading enemy fires. Agility has two time components: (1) the time required for the unit to clear its current site (t_c), and (2) the time required for the unit to close into its relocation site (t_r). The total time required to relocate is then $T = t_c + t_r$.

Training. The ability of a unit to move quickly is in part affected by its level of training. This is especially true of its ability to clear a site quickly. The relocation time depends partly on the maximum (designed) speed of the unit, f_m, and the distance, E, between the current site to the relocation site, so that $t_r = E/f_m$. If we let r be the training level of the unit ($0 \leq r \leq 1$), then $r = 0$ means the unit is untrained and $r = 1$ means the unit is fully trained. The level of unit training affects the time required to clear a threatened site, as well as the degree to which the unit is able to take advantage of the unit's maximum speed. We assume that t_c and f_m imply fully trained units. The effect of training on the total time to relocate is

$$T' = \frac{1}{r}t_c + \frac{E}{\frac{1}{r}f_m}.$$

For poorly trained units (r close to 0), the time to clear the threatened site increases and the unit is unable to take advantage of the unit's maximum speed. For highly trained units (r close to 1), the time to clear is minimized and the unit speed is maximized.

The enemy. A true metric of force agility in avoiding enemy fires by evasion should include some assessment of enemy intent. If we let t_a be the time enemy fires will begin, then the Blue commander must clear his force from his present site before t_a to avoid enemy fires. If t is current time, then $\Delta t = t_a - t$ is the amount of time available to the Blue commander. We can account for this window in the metric as follows:

$$T' = \left(\Delta t - \frac{t_c}{r} \right) + \frac{rE}{f_m}.$$

In this formulation, it is possible for T' to be negative. This happens whenever the time required to clear the current site exceeds the time available before the enemy strikes. In this case, we conclude that the friendly force was not agile enough to avoid enemy fires. Note, however, that this measure does not indicate whether the unit was destroyed. That is covered in other measures and metrics.

Knowledge. Information affects the agility metric in two ways: (1) it provides the friendly commander with advanced information on the timing of the enemy attack, thereby increasing his warning time, Δt, and (2) it provides information on a suitable relocation site nearest to the friendly unit's current location, thereby reducing the time required to relocate, t_r. The lack of information has the opposite effect on each of these components. The knowledge metric, Γ, can be used again to develop a factor that adds these effects to T'. Recall that if $0 \le \Gamma < 1$, Red has information superiority, and if $\Gamma > 1$, Blue has information superiority. If $\Gamma = 1$, Red and Blue have achieved information parity.

Warning. Information has a direct effect on the amount of warning time Δt available to the Blue commander. If Red enjoys information superiority, we would expect that the effect would be to decrease Δt. It would take longer for the Blue commander to discern the enemy's intent and thus shrink his warning time. Conversely, if Blue has information superiority, we would expect that the Blue commander would detect enemy intentions earlier and therefore increase his warning time. If information parity exists, we would expect no effect on warning time.

Consider the function, $f(\Gamma) = e^{1-\Gamma}$, depicted in Figure 6.13. It produces a factor ranging from 0 to e that varies with knowledge. The curve has the desired effect of producing a factor that exceeds 1 whenever $\Gamma < 1$, equals 1 whenever $\Gamma = 1$, and is less than 1 whenever $\Gamma > 1$. The revised mobility factor now accounting for the effects of information becomes

$$T' = \left(\frac{\Delta t}{f(\Gamma)} - \frac{t_c}{r} \right) + \frac{f(\Gamma)rE}{f_m}.$$

RAND *MR1155-A-6.13*

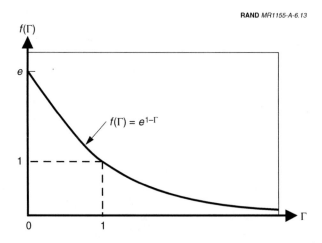

Figure 6.13—Warning Time Factor

We apply the warning-time factor to the time to relocate as well, since the effect we desire also applies there. If $0 \le \Gamma < 1$, then $1 < f(\Gamma) \le e$. The effect we desire under these conditions is a reduced warning time. The fraction $\dfrac{\Delta t}{f(\Gamma)}$ achieves this effect. Similarly, under the same conditions (Red information superiority), we would expect an increase in closure time, and therefore multiplying the closure time $\dfrac{rE}{f_m}$ by $f(\Gamma)$ achieves the desired effect. If Blue and Red are at information parity, $\Gamma = 1$, then $f(\Gamma) = 1$ and the factor has no effect on the agility metric. If Blue has information superiority, $\Gamma > 1$, then $1 < f(\Gamma) < 0$. This has the effect of increasing warning time and decreasing closure time as desired.

Figure 6.14 illustrates the major effects. For both curves, the time to clear the threatened site is taken to be 1.5 hours, the distance to the relocation site is 20 miles, and the maximum unit speed is 20 mph. The left side of the figure illustrates the effects of poor training. Note that the relative knowledge score must exceed 2 before the unit has sufficient time to relocate (recall that the first term of the mobility metric is negative when the time to clear the threatened site exceeds the warning time). In the right side of Figure 6.14, the well-trained unit always has time to relocate.

RAND *MR1155-A-6.14*

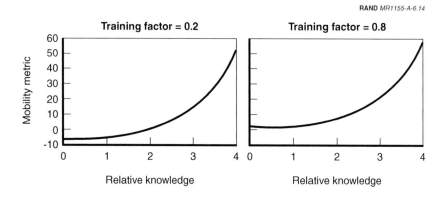

Figure 6.14—Mobility Metric

Chapter Seven

MOEs FOR STABILITY AND SUPPORT OPERATIONS

In this chapter we examine some new measures for military operations other than war (MOOTW), commonly referred to in the Army as "smaller-scale contingency operations" (SSC) or "Stability and Support Operations." According to current joint doctrine, there are sixteen contingency types within the category of MOOTW (Table 7.1). These range from a simple show-of-force operation to more complex undertakings such as support to counterinsurgency and strikes and raids. Land forces would deal with most of the contingency types. A few, like protection of shipping, enforcing exclusion zones, and ensuring freedom of navigation, would chiefly be the responsibility of naval and air forces.

Table 7.1

MOOTW Contingencies

Arms control	Nation assistance/support to counterinsurgency
Combating terrorism	NEO
Counter drug operations	Peace operations
Sanctions enforcement	Protection of shipping
Enforcing exclusion zones	Recovery operations
Ensuring freedom of navigation	Show of force operations
Humanitarian assistance	Strikes and raids
Military support to civilian authorities	Support to insurgency

SOURCE: Joint Pub 3-07.

There have been few serious attempts to identify meaningful MOEs for these operations, and fewer attempts to develop metrics for the MOEs.[1] Given that a reasonable measure can be agreed upon, it is usually framed as a qualitative attribute (later we explore "understanding" as a measure, for example). Developing a metric then means applying quantitative value to qualitative measures. It is easy to lose credibility when assigning numbers to what are essentially ideas. Nevertheless, we proceed with caution and illustrate the process for one contingency type, namely, humanitarian assistance operations.

THE CHANGING NATURE OF ASSISTANCE OPERATIONS

Humanitarian assistance operations in the 2020 timeframe will differ somewhat from those of today. Some of the changes will be of scale rather than of type. Overall, the basic tasks required of the U.S. Army will remain the same, but the changes in the nature of assistance operations will make some of those tasks more difficult.

For example, in the current era most assistance operations have taken place in rural settings, but we can expect a significant portion of these operations in 2020 to be conducted in the sprawling urban areas of the developing world. As large population increases overtax rural agricultural regions, more and more residents of the developing world will migrate to the cities in search of employment. The resulting strain on urban infrastructures can already be seen today in cities like Cairo, Lima, and Mexico City. Political strife or a natural disaster could cut off reliable food deliveries into a large urban area, causing a humanitarian disaster. In 2020, such events may force the Army to

---

[1]One serious attempt currently ongoing was reported in A. Nicholls, "Developing and Using Metrics and Measures of Effectiveness for the Analysis of Smaller-Scale Contingency Operations," in *Proceedings of the 10th ROK-US Defense Analysis Seminar*, 1999. The author reports on work sponsored by the DOD Office of the Director, Programs Analysis and Evaluation, to develop an analytic framework for assessing SSC programmatic issues. The work starts with a top-down study of SRCs much like a Strategy-to-Task methodology developed at RAND (Pirnie and Gardiner, 1996). At each level in the hierarchy, relationships are identified and metrics are defined. The model is time-phased and therefore PERT-like relationships are established as well (PERT is Program Evaluation Review Technique). Output from the process consists of time series charts with the metrics as dependent variables.

marry urban security tactics with urban infrastructure restoration on a large scale.

International media coverage of the U.S. Army in assistance operations will only increase and intensify as we move into the AAN era. The proliferation of commercial communications satellites, Internet access, and global TV news organizations will cast an ever brighter glare of media exposure upon the Army's role. It will be important for the Army to stand up well to this scrutiny without resorting to censorship or large-scale news blackouts. Conveying a positive image of its role in humanitarian assistance operations may be one of the most important tasks for the Army of 2020 to achieve in the realm of MOOTW.

The Army's humanitarian assistance operations of the 1990s have caused it to work alongside a wide array of relief groups (NGOs, PVOs), foreign militaries, supranational organizations (e.g., the UN), and local political factions. In 2020, these operations will be conducted in an even more diverse political environment. New types of transnational business and environmental groups will emerge and have a stake in the potential success (or failure) of an operation. The Army will have to remain flexible enough in its thinking to deal with such actors even-handedly without having to sacrifice American national objectives.

In the 2020 timeframe, the physical environment will most likely present more challenges to humanitarian assistance operations as well. Two contingencies that stand out are epidemics and WMD contamination. Indeed, each could well serve as the triggering event for a large assistance operation. Medical experts are growing increasingly concerned about the increase in outbreaks of deadly infectious diseases (e.g., Ebola) that resist existing drugs. The risk is especially severe in countries where public health networks are weak or nonexistent. In recent years, there have been a number of serious "mini-epidemics" in central Africa. A more serious outbreak could devastate an entire region, forcing the international community to respond with a large-scale humanitarian assistance operation, one in which the U.S. Army, because of its broad capabilities, might be asked to play a role.

Furthermore, the proliferation of WMD in the developing world by 2020 raises the specter of some regional conflicts involving large-scale exchanges of nuclear, biological, or chemical weapons. Such exchanges would leave behind zones of devastation, in which the international community might be forced to intervene. Once again, the U.S. Army could find itself involved in such endeavors. Both types of "dirty environment" contingencies would certainly require the Army to possess a much more robust force protection capability than it has today.

Finally, in 2020 one can expect most humanitarian assistance operations to be organized by ad hoc international coalitions or regional security organizations. The UN, while still exercising authority over some assistance operations, will probably be too hampered by its sheer size and financial problems to tackle the most demanding and dangerous operations.

MOEs FOR HUMANITARIAN ASSISTANCE OPERATIONS

We chose humanitarian assistance as our key "case study" for three reasons. First, the Army has had a fair amount of recent experience in conducting such operations. American interventions in Somalia, Haiti, and Rwanda each included an assistance component and thus provide a database of lessons learned that can be put to use in the process of devising MOEs.

Second, humanitarian assistance operations involve a rich mix of political and military means used to achieve logistical ends, a mix possibly more complicated than in other types of MOOTW. Ultimately, the success or failure of assistance operations depends on both creating an orderly environment free of outlaw activity and restoring the local infrastructure to a level at which sufficient relief supplies can flow to afflicted areas.

Third, we chose a case study of humanitarian assistance operations because they compel the Army to work alongside many different types of actors (NGOs, PVOs, foreign militaries, journalists, etc.).

We use the four operational concepts from *Joint Vision 2010* to organize the MOEs for humanitarian assistance. A total of thirteen MOEs are presented in Table 7.2. Of these, we chose to develop the

Table 7.2

Humanitarian Assistance MOEs

Operational Concept	Measure of Effectiveness
Dominant maneuver	Understanding local environment Infrastructure restoration Information management Interagency, multinational relations Civil order
Precision engagement	People affected Resource flow
Full-dimensional protection	Casualties Force protection against hostile factions Protection of relief populations against hostile factions Protection from environmental effects
Focused logistics	Timely support Tonnage

first MOE, "understanding the local environment," to illustrate the process as an example or prototype of what could also be done for the other candidate measures listed in the table.

METRICS FOR HUMANITARIAN ASSISTANCE OPERATIONS

The difficulty in attempting to apply quantitative metrics to qualitative measures is compounded in the case of humanitarian assistance because few of the traditional warfighting metrics apply. In fact, there is rarely a well-defined enemy, and therefore the environment in the host nation becomes the surrogate enemy. As a result, the metrics are generally one-sided. That is, we focus more on the ability of the Blue force to operate in a multinational coalition environment and not on how well the force can operate relative to an enemy force.

Table 7.3 lists the metrics for humanitarian assistance in the usual format. We have restricted our discussion to only one of the measures in the *dominant maneuver* category, namely, "understanding the local environment" and its corresponding metric "contribution of knowledge to degree of understanding." This measure has been

Table 7.3

Dominant Maneuver in Humanitarian Assistance

MOE	Traditional Metric	Information-Age Metric
Understanding the local environment	Amount of accurate intelligence distributed	Contribution of knowledge to the degree of understanding
Infrastructure restoration	Square miles rebuilt	—
Interagency, multinational relations	Percent total positive news coverage	

chosen to demonstrate the process of arguing from qualitative measures to quantitative and quasi-quantitative metrics. Unlike combat metrics, humanitarian assistance metrics depend almost completely upon the specific operation being analyzed. Nevertheless, we shall attempt to develop some first principles.

UNDERSTANDING THE LOCAL ENVIRONMENT

Understanding the local environment is a primary concern when engaging in humanitarian assistance operations. The several components of the environment listed in Table 7.4 illustrate why understanding is so important. Stated as a measure of effectiveness, we wish to measure the degree to which U.S. forces participating in humanitarian assistance operation *understand* the local environment. The assumption is that the more that is understood, the less likely the forces are to alienate the indigenous population, their leaders, relief organizations also participating in the operation, and the U.S. national and international community.

Table 7.4 lists the constituent components of the "local environment." It is impossible to compile a list like this that is exhaustive. What we depict here is one that appears to cover most types of humanitarian assistance operations. These components are not equally important to the success of an operation, and the ranking will vary with the operation. A logical context-free ranking might be as illustrated by the component groups in the table. Power is more important than customs, which in turn are more important than the physical environment. Although we suggest that this ordering is

Table 7.4

Local Environment

Component Group	Ranking	Constituent Component
Power	1	Levers of power
	2	Local politics
	3	Local government
Customs	4	Culture
	5	History
Physical Environment	6	Terrain
	7	Weather

"context free," an argument can be made that it might be "context dependent" in certain cases. In either case, the metric development process described below applies.

Metrics

A metric that reflects the "level of understanding" in these three broad categories is extremely problematic. The question is, "What constitutes understanding?" One way to deal with this dilemma is to ignore it and proceed as follows. Suppose we let U_i be the condition "component group i is understood." That is,

- U_1 = "power relationships in the host nation are understood."

- U_2 = "host nation customs are understood."

- U_3 = "the host nation's physical environment is understood."

This allows us to establish a simple binary relation for each component group. Either the commander of the operation understands the group (U_i) or he does not ($\overline{U}_i$). That is, we ignore the "level" of understanding and rely instead on the commander's assessment. If he (or more accurately, his planners) feels that he has enough understanding, then we assess his state as U_i.

The ordinal *importance* ranking of the constituent component groups, $1 \succ 2 \succ 3$, helps us to assess the commander's understanding of the local environment. The rule decision tree depicted in Figure 7.1 summarizes the process of assessing understanding. At every node, a U_i or $\overline{U}_i$ branch leads either to the next group of components or to a terminus. The assessment that a component group is understood is subjective, or it can be a simple rule such as *"if the number of components in a component group that are understood exceeds a threshold, then the component group is understood."* In Figure 7.1, this is represented as decision blocks such as $P \geq 2$. If the number of power components understood is two or more, then this component group is assessed to be sufficiently understood to proceed to examining the next component group in order.

The diagram is an aid to assessing our level of understanding. First, if we do not understand the power structure, whatever else we understand is obviated and we assess our understanding to be insufficient ($\overline{S}$). If we understand the power structure but nothing else, we again assess our understanding to be insufficient. For all other cases, we assess our understanding to be sufficient (S).

Knowledge

Knowledge can help understanding and therefore improve the two cases where our understanding is assessed to be insufficient. There

RAND *MR1155-A-7.1*

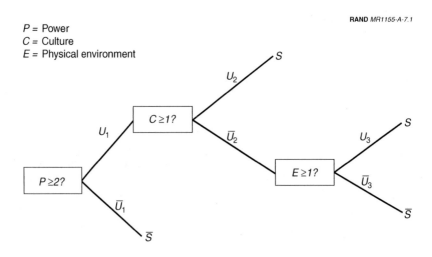

P = Power
C = Culture
E = Physical environment

Figure 7.1—Assessing Understanding

are several sources of knowledge in humanitarian assistance operations, and they will certainly vary with the mission. Table 7.5 lists a few that might be considered context free.

With the exception of AAN technology sensors, all the sources listed in the table are available to us now. However, we would expect the processing of information from these sources to improve considerably by the AAN timeframe.

Unlike combat MOEs, a relative score for knowledge is not practical, in that there is no "enemy" in the traditional sense. Consequently, our metric must be one-sided. One way we can build a simple metric is to focus on the assessment of the *availability* of information from the various sources about each of the constituent components. If we let $s_{i,j}$ be the availability of information about component j from source i, then we can establish the simple binary relation

$$s_{i,j} = \begin{cases} 1 \text{ if information about } i \text{ from source } j \text{ is available} \\ 0 \text{ if it is not} . \end{cases}$$

For example, if we have information about "levers of power" from local officials, then $s_{1,3} = 1$. This formulation is strictly binary. That is, we make no assessment of the quantity or quality of the information available or, for that matter, the appropriateness of using information about levers of power obtained from local officials. However,

Table 7.5

Information Sources

Rank	Source
1	AAN technology sensor systems
2	Local officials
3	Special Operations Forces
4	Historical documents
5	Relief agencies
6	Foreign governments/nationals
7	News agencies
8	International and regional NGOs
9	Other

RAND *MR1155-A-7.2*

Components

$$R = \begin{bmatrix} r_{1,1} & r_{1,2} & r_{1,3} & r_{1,4} & r_{1,5} & r_{1,6} & r_{1,7} \\ r_{2,1} & & & & & & \cdot \\ r_{3,1} & \cdot & & & & & \cdot \\ r_{4,1} & & & & & & \cdot \\ r_{5,1} & & \cdot & & & & \cdot \\ r_{6,1} & & & \cdot & & & \cdot \\ r_{7,1} & & & & & & \cdot \\ r_{8,1} & & & & \cdot & & \cdot \\ r_{9,1} & \cdot & \cdot & & \cdot & \cdot & r_{9,7} \end{bmatrix}$$

(Sources)

Figure 7.2—Source Reliability Matrix

some sources will be more reliable than others, and some will be more reliable when reporting on some components than on others. This suggests a "reliability" matrix that reflects this phenomenon such as depicted in Figure 7.2. The seven components of the local environment are organized as columns and the sources are listed as rows. For example, $r_{1,3}$ is the reliability of local officials when reporting on levers of power. The situation may be such that local officials are assessed to be highly reliable when reporting about levers of power, so $r_{1,3}$ would be assessed to be very high.

In any case, the $r_{i,j}$ are restricted to values between 0 and 1. Our knowledge about local environment component j, then, can be expressed as

$$k_j = \sum_i r_{i,j} s_{i,j}.$$

A perfect score in this case would be $k_j = 9$. That is, a 9 would be achieved if reports are available from all sources ($s_{i,j} = 1$ for all i) and the reliability of all sources when reporting on component j is 1 ($r_{i,j} = 1$ for all i). This allows us to normalize the knowledge metric to obtain

$$\|k_j\| = \frac{k_j}{9}.$$

Knowledge gives us confidence that we understand the component more fully. For example, suppose that in applying the process described in Figure 7.1, we assess our understanding of local politics to be insufficient to contribute to our understanding of power in the region, $(\bar{u}_1)$.[2] The knowledge factor $\|k_1\|$ does not increase our knowledge about the component, but rather it reflects the degree to which the knowledge we possess constitutes understanding. This is based on the fact that $\|k_j\|$ evaluates the sources of our knowledge and the reliability we place on them. This suggests a knowledge-enhanced rule set for each of the constituent local environment components:

1. If $u_j \cap (\|k_j\| > \alpha)$, then u_j

2. If $u_j \cap (\|k_j\| \leq \alpha)$, then $\bar{u}_j$

3. If $\bar{u}_j \cap (\|k_j\| > \beta)$, then u_j

4. If $\bar{u}_j \cap (\|k_j\| \leq \beta)$, then $\bar{u}_j$.

These rules are logic statements. For example, Rule 1 is read "if component j is considered to be understood, and the reliability of sources reporting on component j exceeds a threshold α, then component j is assessed to be sufficiently understood." The threshold values α and β are numbers set to be between 0 and 1. It is not necessary that they be equal, in that we would expect the requirement to change from "understanding" (u) to "not understanding" $(\bar{u})$ to be different from the reverse requirement.

---

[2]The lowercase u is used here to represent understanding of the individual components of the component group.

Chapter Eight

CONCLUDING OBSERVATIONS AND
POTENTIAL IMPLICATIONS

The critical variable for determining the contours of the Information-Age Army is information. The degree of information superiority that one side might be able to achieve over the other is, potentially, what most needs to be measured for effectiveness in the Information Age.

Furthermore, as argued in earlier chapters of this report, gaining knowledge is as much a contest as is maneuver or the effective application of firepower in military operations. Thus, we have focused here on relative measures beginning with relative knowledge, for which we developed the knowledge metric. This metric expresses the relationship between ideal and actual knowledge, for both sides, in military operations.

Information superiority can be thought of, analytically, as the outcome of a two-sided interaction between opponents (i.e., a game or contest), in which one side achieves a decisive advantage, or some degree of dominance, over the other. In the extreme or best case, the superior side enjoys perfect information on both its own and its opponent's forces, as well as perfect intelligence about the opponent—including knowledge of the opponent's plans, intentions, and choices almost as soon as the opponent has decided to act upon them; it can even include the ability to affect what the opponent knows. In short, the superior side achieves "information dominance."

The high degree of superiority that one side can conceivably obtain over another in the Information Age is what makes this variable, on the one hand, so critical and potentially revolutionary. On the other hand, if neither side can achieve information dominance over the other—or even significant degrees of information superiority—the technologies of the Information Age and their much-heralded benefits may not prove to be as one-sided or decisive, for either side, as enthusiasts tend to assume. First and foremost among MOEs for the Army of the future, therefore, are those that measure how to achieve and maintain information superiority and, if possible, information dominance.

The quest for information superiority leading to dominance might also change the nature of land power and ground warfare in the future. The direction of this change, as the Army evolves from its current force structure to Army XXI and, beyond that, to the AAN, could result in a reconfiguration of current relationships between firepower and maneuver on the battlefield. The historical balance between firepower and maneuver, which tended to favor firepower throughout much of the 20th century, could change, thanks largely to the role of information versus other technologies and systems.

By the time the AAN arrives in 2025 or beyond, Information-Age developments might already have enabled Army maneuver units to fight dispersed across both the length and the depth of future battlefields. In other words, ground forces may no longer measure success or failure by their ability to maintain a continuous FLOT but, rather, by the amount of both immediate and surrounding battlespace a given unit can control at a particular time. Even if FLOT movement continues to endure as an important yardstick, measuring it will be affected by the role that information plays in such calculations. The ability to maneuver ground units more effectively than at present (to maximize their operational reach) is what Information-Age technologies promise to provide.

Measuring the effectiveness of forces in combat, therefore, will remain a central focus for the Army in the Information Age. Only in the most extreme case—such total information dominance over an enemy that he chooses not to fight at all—is Information-Age warfare likely to obviate the need for combat. More likely, it seems, is a future characterized by contests in which information superiority is at issue, with both sides competing for it in dynamic fashion (e.g., through measures taken as initiatives and countermeasures launched in response) and the outcome being decided by force of arms. In the Information Age, however, such combat outcomes seem likely to bear a strong positive relationship to the contributions that new technologies of the era, including but not limited to information technologies, can make to warfare. Hence, new MOEs, like the ones we have posited in this report, are needed to gauge the effectiveness of the new technologies' contributions to combat.

Finally, security and stability operations, formerly known as military operations other than war (MOOTW), will continue to function as significant claimants on the need for and use of military forces. Measuring the effectiveness of forces employed in this context is no mean feat, whether at present, in the recent past, or during the Information-Age future. But measure we must, in terms that are relevant to the new future and its technological promises. We have tried to suggest here not only that such measurements are necessary, because of the continuing role that security and stability operations will play in the future, but also that new MOEs tailored to MOOTW-like missions and Information-Age technologies are possible. We believe they can actually be established for the Information Age, not least because they can be constructed in ways that conform in important respects to the MOEs we have postulated for Information-Age combat.

REFERENCES

Army Vision 2010, Department of the Army, undated.

Arquilla, J., *Dubious Battles: Aggression, Defeat, and the International System,* RAND Research Study, Washington, D.C.: Crane Russak, 1992.

Arquilla, J. and D. Ronfeldt, "Cyberwar is Coming," *Comparative Strategy,* Vol. 12, 1993, pp. 141–165.

Blahut, R. E., *Principles and Practice of Information Theory,* Reading, MA: Addison-Wesley, 1988.

Bracken, J., "Lanchester Models of the Ardennes Campaign," *Naval Research Logistics,* Vol. 42, 1995, pp. 559–577.

Bracken, J. (ed.), *Combat Models,* John Wiley, 1995.

Concept for Future Joint Operations: Expanding Joint Vision 2010, Department of Defense, May 1997.

Davis, P. K., and J. K. Bigelow, *Experiments in Multiresolution Modeling (MRM),* Santa Monica, CA: RAND, MR-1004-DARPA, 1998.

Davis, P. K., D. Blumenthal, and D. Gaver, "Combat Modeling Issues," Appendix I in *Technology for the United States Navy and Marine Corps, 2000–2035,* National Academy Press, Vol. 9, 1997.

Deitchman, S. J., "A Lanchester Model of Guerrilla Warfare," *Journal of the Operations Research Society of America,* Vol. 10, 1962, pp. 818–827.

Fisher, R. A., "Theory of Statistical Estimation," in *Proceedings of the Cambridge Philosophical. Society,* Vol. 22, 1925, pp. 700–725.

Ford, L. R., Jr., and D. R. Fulkerson, *Flows in Networks,* Princeton, NJ: Princeton University Press, 1962.

Gritton, E.C., P. K. Davis, R. Steeb, and J. Matsumura, *Ground Forces for a Rapidly Employable Joint Task Force: First-Week Capabilities for Short-Warning Conflicts,* Santa Monica, CA: RAND, MR-1152.0, 1999.

Hartley, R. V. L., "Transmission of Information," *Bell System Technical Journal,* Vol. 7, 1928, p. 535.

Joint Staff, *Joint Doctrine for Information Operations,* JCS Publication 3-13, October 1998.

Lanchester, F. W., *Aircraft in Warfare: The Dawn of the Fourth Arm,* London: Constable and Co., 1916. Reprinted in J. Newman (ed.), *The World of Mathematics,* Vol. 4, New York: Simon and Schuster, 1956.

Luce, R. D., and H. Raiffa, *Games and Decisions,* New York: Wiley, 1957.

Nicholls, A., "Developing and Using Metrics and Measures of Effectiveness for the Analysis of Smaller-Scale Contingency Operations," *Proceedings of the 10th ROK-US Defense Analysis Seminar,* Seoul, Korea, 1999.

Nyquist, H., "Certain Factors Affecting Telegraph Speed," *Bell System Technical Journal,* Vol. 3, 1924, p. 324.

Perry, W., and M. Millot, *Army After Next: Winter Wargame Issues,* Santa Monica, CA: RAND, MR-988-A, 1998.

Perry, W., and J. Moffat, "Measuring the Effect of Knowledge in Military Campaigns," *Journal of the Operational Research Society* (UK), Vol. 48, No. 10, 1997, pp. 965–972.

Perry, W., B. Pirnie, and J. Gordon, *The Future of Warfare: A Report on the 1999 Army After Next Study Cycle,* Santa Monica, CA: RAND, MR-1156-A, 1999a.

Perry, W., B. Pirnie, and J. Gordon, *Issues Raised During the 1998 Army After Next Spring Wargame,* Santa Monica, CA: RAND, MR-1023-A, 1999b.

Pirnie, B., and Gardiner, S. *An Objectives-Based Approach to Military Campaign Analysis,* Santa Monica, CA: RAND, MR-656-JS, 1996.

Shannon, C. E., "A Mathematical Theory of Communication," *Bell System Technical Journal,* Vol. 27, 1948, pp. 379–423 and 623–656.

Smith, D. G., "The Probability Distribution of the Number of Survivors in a Two-Sided Combat Situation," *Journal of the Operational Research Society* (UK), Vol. 49, 1997.

Taylor, James G., *Lanchester Models of Warfare,* 2 vols., Military Applications Section, Operations Research Society of America, 1983.

U.S. Department of the Army, *Force XXI Operations: A Concept for the Evolution of Full-Dimensional Operations for the Strategic Army of the Early Twenty-First Century,* Fort Monroe, VA: Headquarters, U.S. Army Training and Doctrine Command, TRADOC Pamphlet 525-5, August 1, 1994.

U.S. Department of the Army, *Information Operations,* Field Manual 100-6, 1996.

U.S. Department of the Army, *Knowledge and Speed: The Annual Report on The Army After Next Project to the Chief of Staff of the Army,* Fort Monroe, VA: Headquarters, U.S. Army Training and Doctrine Command, July 1997.

U.S. Department of the Army, *Knowledge and Speed: Battle Force and the U.S. Army of 2025, The 1998 Annual Report on the Army After Next Project to the Chief of Staff of the Army,* Fort Monroe, VA: Headquarters, U.S. Army Training and Doctrine Command, December 1998.

U.S. Department of Defense, *Conduct of the Persian Gulf War,* Report to Congress, Washington, D.C., 1992.

U.S. Department of Defense, *Joint Vision 2010,* available at Web site *http://www.dtic.mil/jv2020/history.htm* (site accessed and running on November 27, 2000).

U.S. Department of Defense, *Joint Vision 2020,* available at Web site *http://www.dtic.mil/jv2020/jvpub2.htm* (site accessed and running on November 27, 2000).

Wagner, H. M., *Principles of Operations Research, With Applications to Managerial Decisions,* Englewood Cliffs, NJ: Prentice Hall, 1969.

Washburn, A. R., *Bits, Bangs or Bucks? The Coming Information Crisis,* Naval Postgraduate School Paper at *http://web.nps.navy.mil/~orfacpag/resumePages/washburn/infoval.pdf.* (Web page was accessed and available on October 19, 2000.)